CAT
& Kitten
CARE

CAT

&

Kitten

CARE

A COMPREHENSIVE GUIDE TO THE CARE AND WELFARE OF YOUR PET

Paddy Cutts

Colour Library

In memory of two special cats, Mompuss and Trotter

CLB 4890

First published 1996 by Colour Library Direct

Godalming, Surrey, United Kingdom

Photographs © 1996 Animals Unlimited

ISBN 1-85833-553-1

Conceived and produced by Linda Doeser Publishing Services
Editorial Director: Linda Doeser
Editorial Assistant: Ann Dean
Veterinary Consultant: John Oliver, BVETMED, MRCVS
Illustrations: Samantha Elmhurst

Design by Kingfisher Design, London
Art Director: Pedro Prá-Lopez
Designers: Frank Landamore, Frances Prá-Lopez

Printed and bound in Italy

Cover design: CLB International

CONTENTS

INTRODUCTION

In this book I have tried to help you find your way through all the many pleasures and responsibilities of choosing, buying and caring for a cat. Think of the process as being rather like having a family car. First you must choose the right model – one that matches your lifestyle and needs. You provide it with fuel to keep it going and proper cleaning maintains its bodywork. Regular servicing ensures that it purrs along smoothly and that minor problems can be addressed before they become major and incapacitating. When it is getting older, it needs more nursing along and more frequent servicing. With this kind of care, your car – or your cat – will provide years of pleasure.

You cannot think too hard or too long before choosing your cat. You would be astonished to learn how many cats and kittens pass through animal sanctuaries or are re-homed by the many cat rescue societies simply because their original purchasers did not take enough time or seek enough advice to make an informed decision. A cat bought on the spur of the moment could turn out to be one of the worst decisions you ever make.

First of all, you must make absolutely sure that the type or breed of cat you choose will fit in with all the family's wishes and needs. Do you want a pedigree or, perhaps, non-pedigree, a male or female, a 'talkative' cat, or even more than one cat? Do not forget that longhairs will require more time spent on grooming and will shed more hairs on your carpets and furniture. Given that there are more than 100 recognized cat breeds, you are certainly spoilt for choice. However, do not think that you will like every single breed. Just like people, the looks and personality of a particular breed might have tremendous appeal for one family, while another may find them distinctly off-putting.

Having considered all the general pros and cons and your family's specific needs, remember finally that you will probably be gaining a devoted companion for maybe 18 years or longer, who will be totally dependent on you for food, friendship, grooming, health care, amusement and, most of all, love. If you can provide these in full measure, everything you expect from your cat will come back to you, many times over.

Choosing a kitten is an important decision. With proper care and some good fortune, it will probably be sharing your home and your life almost as long as a child would.

I

THE NEW KITTEN

I t is a common misconception that the best place to find a new kitten is a pet shop, but please think again – after all, you would hardly expect baby stores to stock babies, would you?

Fortunately, few reputable pet shops now sell livestock, other than birds and fish, as they recognize that a shop is not a suitable environment for baby animals, such as kittens and puppies. The sad few that do end up in such establishments are usually far too young to have

left their mothers, are prone to infection, as they will not be old enough to have had all the necessary inoculations and, in the case of pedigree animals, are often the runts of a litter that a breeder has been unable to 'off load' elsewhere. Use your pet shop purely as a 'shop window'; many carry notices for kittens looking for good homes and some may even know of reputable breeders of pedigree kittens with whom they can put you in touch.

WHERE TO FIND YOUR KITTEN

Most often, the best way of acquiring a kitten is by word of mouth. You may have friends with a pedigree breed whose temperament and looks you like. They will be able to tell you how to contact the breeder from whom they bought their kitten.

You may also know of someone whose non-pedigree female cat has been mated and is looking for homes for the offspring.

If this is not practicable, the following may help you find the kitten you require:
• notice board in the local veterinary practice
• advertisements in local newspaper
• advertisements in local shop windows
• advertisements in the national press
• advertisements in specialist cat magazines
• cat and general animal charities
• kitten list from breed cat clubs
• for a pedigree breed – go to a cat show and see all the varieties available and talk with the breeders

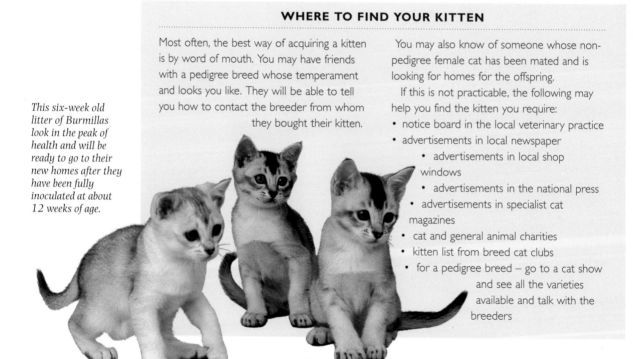

This six-week old litter of Burmillas look in the peak of health and will be ready to go to their new homes after they have been fully inoculated at about 12 weeks of age.

Warning

It is rare for a father that is a resident in the feline family to attack his offspring, but this is not usually the case with an intruding tom. Kittens should never be left unsupervised or unprotected outdoors.

Sometimes the father may show an interest in his offspring, but he still leaves the serious duties to the mother.

PEDIGREE OR NON-PEDIGREE?

Cats, whether pedigree or not, can live for a very long time – 18 years or more is not unknown – so it is of the utmost importance that you make the right choice in the first place. Sadly, some people take on a cat or kitten as a 'spur of the moment' decision and, if things do not work out, the poor creature will end up in a rescue agency as another unwanted pet. This is one of the reasons why breeders and rescue centres interview prospective owners so carefully.

Your decision to share your life with a cat is a very personal one – and the whole family should be involved in the final choice. Never give a kitten as a birthday or Christmas present unless you are absolutely sure that it is wanted.

If you are thinking of having a kitten simply as a pet, you may prefer a 'moggie'. If you also aspire to showing your cat, remember that most cat shows have a section for cats of unknown parentage. The cat will be with you for about as long as a child would stay at home, so let's weigh up the pros and cons for both types of cat.

The pedigree Siamese on the right is a known-quantity and its adult personality, size and shape could have been predicted with considerable accuracy. The non-pedigree on the left has grown into something of a gentle giant, but its adult size, chunky shape and sweet nature were not necessarily apparent when it was a kitten.

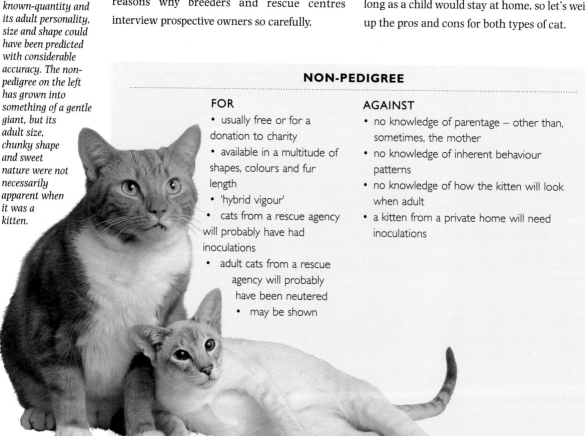

NON-PEDIGREE

FOR
- usually free or for a donation to charity
- available in a multitude of shapes, colours and fur length
- 'hybrid vigour'
- cats from a rescue agency will probably have had inoculations
- adult cats from a rescue agency will probably have been neutered
- may be shown

AGAINST
- no knowledge of parentage – other than, sometimes, the mother
- no knowledge of inherent behaviour patterns
- no knowledge of how the kitten will look when adult
- a kitten from a private home will need inoculations

PEDIGREE

FOR

- available in a huge variety of colours, shapes and sizes, including the newer 'designer' breeds
- known family background and inherent personality and character traits
- known size and shape of the adult cat
- kittens will have had their full course of inoculations
- may be shown and bred from (if no restrictions on registration document)
- price tag includes inoculations, veterinary check, worming and, frequently, insurance
- access to advice and information from an experienced reputable breeder

AGAINST

- can cost a lot of money (usually £150/$240 or more)
- some pedigree breeds are a lot more demanding than others
- may need specialist grooming care

One of the newer and increasingly popular pedigree breeds is the Bengal.

BREEDERS

Quite often, owners of pedigree cats are also breeders – they do this as a hobby, albeit an expensive one, rather than a business. If you are contemplating buying a pedigree kitten, go direct to the breeder; most advertise their kittens in specialist cat magazines and journals and regularly attend cat shows, which are always a good starting point. Do not be influenced by the number of cats they have or the prize-winning trophies and rosettes on display. What is important is that the kittens they produce are happy, healthy and used to a normal household routine – most kittens they sell are destined to become household pets and not 'breeding stock'.

If you are seeking a pedigree pet to live in your home, choose one that is used to regular human contact – look for a 'front parlour breeder' rather than a 'battery cattery'!

Most breeders are busy people, often with a job to hold down as well as the responsibilities of a family and home to run, so do give them the following considerations.

- Telephone first for an appointment.
- Do not treat the first visit as a 'trip to the zoo' – leave the children behind!
- Make sure that you see the mother with her kittens.
- Do not be surprised if you are not allowed to handle the kittens – they are very vulnerable before they have been inoculated.
- Do not make appointments to see several breeders on one day. It is just possible that you could carry a feline infection from one household to another.

Doing your homework

If you are not sure what breed would suit your lifestyle, nothing beats visiting an all-breed cat show and actually seeing the different types and varieties – and there are more than 100. Breeders and owners are usually very willing to talk about the finer points of their particular breed and will offer useful advice and information. In the U.K. cat shows are purely shop windows, but in the United States, you can buy cats direct from a show.

*To identify the sex of
your kitten, consult
these illustrations.
While the testicles
are not always
obvious in a very
young kitten, the two
openings are further
apart in a male than
in a female.*

THE RIGHT CAT

Most kittens are destined to become the much-loved family pet and so, unless you are contemplating purchasing a pedigree kitten for breeding purposes, there is little to choose between a male and a female. When grown up and neutered, both will be friendly and affectionate. The only differences are that the males tend to grow to be larger than the females and the cost of neutering is cheaper for a castration than it is for a spay.

One or Two Kittens?

Unless you already have a pet in your home, the answer should be two – especially if you are out at work for most of the day. Two kittens are twice the fun, will keep each other occupied when you are out and cost very little more to keep in the way of food and litter than a single animal. The only extra major cost is that of the annual inoculations. Most people will take at least one

annual holiday and their pets have to be boarded; this can be a lonely experience for a single cat, but two will settle much more quickly, treating their stay in a cattery as a holiday.

Choosing your Kitten

Although there are always exceptions, the personality of a pedigree breed is a known quantity and this is fully explained in Chapter 6 (see page 68). Non-pedigree kittens, often with an unknown father, are not so predictable and their personalities and characters will depend very much on their mother and the environment in which they have been reared.

Personality

It is important to see the kittens in their home with their mother and siblings. This will give you a good indication of how socialized they have become. Be wary if the mother or kittens hiss at you. This may simply be an over-protective mother and the kittens reacting with her, but it could indicate that neither cat nor kittens are used to regular human contact and handling, both of which are extremely important from an early age if the kitten is to integrate into your home as a family pet. Ideally, the whole feline family should be pleased to meet you, with the mother cat proudly showing off her offspring. The kittens should be active, playful, outgoing and interested in all that is going on around them. When choosing your kitten, select a friendly extrovert, rather than one that is timid or shy; the latter may just be of a more retiring disposition, but it could equally suggest behavioural or health problems – or both.

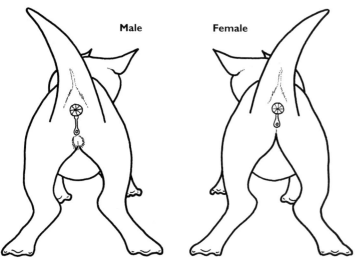

Male   Female

Wherever possible, you should be able to see the kittens with their mother.

HEALTH CHECKS

Pedigree kittens are not sold until they are at least 12 weeks old and will have been checked over by a veterinarian and have received their course of inoculations. This is not always the case with non-pedigrees and many will leave home at eight or nine weeks old without a veterinary inspection or immunization. Look for the following points and you should find that you have a fit and healthy kitten:

• The eyes should be bright and clear, with no sign of weepiness.

• The teeth should be clean and the breath sweet smelling.
• The stomach should be plump but soft: any firmness may denote the presence of worms.
• Look at the litter tray: the motions should be firm and not overly smelly with no sign of diarrhoea.
• The coat should be clean and free of parasites.
• The general appearance should be that of a happy, healthy and well-co-ordinated kitten.

Reminder

When you have collected your new kitten, do not forget its inoculation certificate. Take this to the veterinarian with whom you have registered your cat so that proper records can be kept and a reminder sent when the annual booster shot is due.

PLANNING AHEAD

As with a human baby, your new kitten will require its own special 'layette'. Much of the equipment needed will last a lifetime, so it is not always sensible to buy items such as litter tray or carrying basket in a 'kitten' size, as they will soon grow out of them! Most accessories come in all shapes, styles and sizes, so it is worth going to a good pet shop to see the ranges available.

Finding a Veterinarian

As with most things, personal recommendation is the best way to find a veterinarian. Ask local cat-owning friends who they use and make an appointment for yourself and your new kitten to meet the practitioner. Most practices in urban areas have a small-animal specialist, but in rural areas this may pose more of a problem as the veterinarians will tend more towards the treatment of livestock. If you are buying your kitten from a breeder, ask his advice; the cat fancy is a close network and they will inevitably know of someone with cats in your area who could suggest a good veterinarian for you to use.

It is sensible to register your kitten with the veterinarian as soon as possible. Do not wait for an accident or emergency to arise, as the formalities may delay urgent treatment. Equally, if the veterinarian has already met your kitten when it is healthy and has seen how it normally behaves, it will make it easier for him to diagnose a problem if the kitten is a little unwell and acting unnaturally.

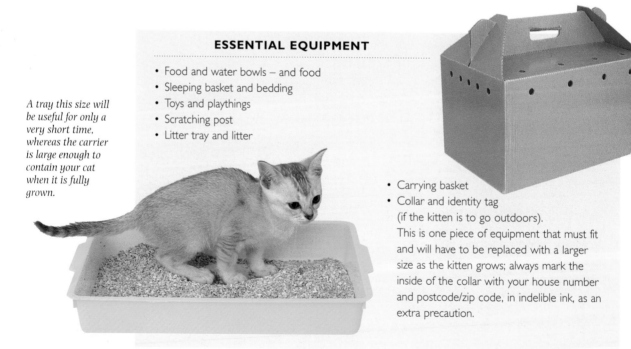

A tray this size will be useful for only a very short time, whereas the carrier is large enough to contain your cat when it is fully grown.

ESSENTIAL EQUIPMENT

- Food and water bowls – and food
- Sleeping basket and bedding
- Toys and playthings
- Scratching post
- Litter tray and litter
- Carrying basket
- Collar and identity tag
  (if the kitten is to go outdoors).
  This is one piece of equipment that must fit and will have to be replaced with a larger size as the kitten grows; always mark the inside of the collar with your house number and postcode/zip code, in indelible ink, as an extra precaution.

SAFETY

'Curiosity killed the cat' is a good adage to remember, especially where kittens are concerned. Cats may be reputed to have nine lives but, when it comes to kittens and the mischief they can get up to, perhaps they should have considerably more! This is particularly true for the first few weeks when a kitten is exploring its new home, so do watch out for the following (especially if you are a first-time cat owner).

- Your feet – it is so easy to tread on a fast-moving kitten.
- Doors – close doors carefully: it is easy to slam a door and hurt or even kill a kitten.
- Cupboards and drawers – kittens are notorious for sleeping in strange places and getting locked in.
- Electrical cables and leads – kittens can chew through them.

- Washing machines, tumble dryers and dishwashers – put a notice on the doors to remind yourself to check before switching the machine on.
- Windows – open windows that are within a kitten's reach should be secured with mesh to prevent accidents.
- Poisonous house plants should be removed or kept out of the kitten's reach.
- Sewing materials, wool and elastic bands – all of these are dangerous to kittens if ingested, so keep them in a safe place.

The list could go on for ever but, in the end, it is a matter of common sense. Think of all the things that could be hazardous to a toddler and take the same precautions for your new kitten – they are both curious young animals!

There are probably more potential dangers to a cat in a kitchen than any other room in the house.

RESCUE CATS

Sadly, there are always unwanted cats looking for new homes, especially early in the year when the novelty of a feline Christmas present has worn off and the poor cat or kitten is abandoned.

There are many other reasons why cats need to be re-homed. Marriages break up and both partners move to smaller premises where it is no longer possible to keep a cat. The 'new baby syndrome' makes the feline 'baby' surplus to requirements when the human version arrives. In times of recession, houses are repossessed and families, including the cat, become homeless. The list could go on and on, but these are all cats that will make good pets as they are not looking for new homes through any fault of their own.

Some cats are re-homed because of behavioural problems; this may be simply that the cat does not like living with other cats, but would make an ideal sole pet. Others may have more undesirable traits, such as aggressive behaviour or anti-social defecation problems. It is, therefore, important to ask why the cat needs

to be re-homed in the first place as you could end up with quite a 'problem puss'.

If you decide to take in a 'rescue', be prepared for the 'third degree' from the re-homing officer. It is always hoped that a cat will be re-homed only once and the questions you will be asked and the follow-on visit can be almost as in-depth as if you were adopting a human baby.

Animal Sanctuaries

These are places that can really pull at your heart strings and the sight of, often, hundreds of abandoned, unwanted pets is enough to make you want to take them all home. On the more positive side, you will be able to see the domestic cat in all its shapes, sizes, colours, patterns and fur length – both pedigree and non-pedigree. Many of these cats have been abandoned because they are pregnant, so you will find many kittens looking for new homes, as well as older adult cats.

All these sanctuaries are run on voluntary donations: if you do decide to adopt a rescue, a contribution to their funds is always appreciated.

RE-HOMED OLDER CATS

Many charities and cat clubs have a list of 'rescues' and there are many good reasons to choose an older cat as a pet. Do not be put off by the cat's age as some will live well into their late teens or even early twenties!

- Usually free to a good home, with a donation to the charity
- Usually well socialized and used to living in a home environment

- Usually neutered and fully inoculated
- Make ideal pets for the older person who could not cope with a highly active kitten
- With pedigrees, the breed club will be able to offer you a pedigree cat without the (often) large price tag that a kitten would command
- With non-pedigrees, the adult size and personality is a known quantity

Never allow your kitten outdoors unsupervised, as its inquisitive nature can get it into situations it cannot get out of on its own.

BRINGING YOUR KITTEN HOME

While you and your family are excited about receiving your new pet, remember this is a traumatic time for the kitten. It is often the first time that it will have been in a car, so do make sure that it feels safe and secure in a suitable carrying basket. Try to ensure that the day you bring the new kitten home is a quiet one. Taking in a kitten at Christmas or for a birthday may be tempting, but such times are usually noisy and will only unnerve the kitten. Try to choose a weekend, perhaps taking a day or two off work either side, so that you will have plenty of time to spare without too many interruptions; this will help you and your new kitten to get to know each other and the kitten to become familiar with its new surroundings.

You should always accompany your cat or kitten when it is first getting used to going outside. You may find it helpful to put on a harness and lead.

Settling In – Indoors

Make sure that you have all the necessary equipment (see page 18) and decide where it will be put. Choose places convenient for both you and the kitten. Cats are creatures of habit and do not appreciate suddenly finding that the litter tray has been moved or they are expected to sleep in a different place.

- Never put the litter tray close to the food and water bowls. Wild cats never soil near where they eat and this is reflected in the behaviour of the domestic cat, so your kitten may choose to defecate elsewhere in your house.
- Choose a warm, draught-free place in a quiet room for sleeping accommodation. If you are tempted to let the kitten sleep in bed with you 'just for the first few nights', think again – this will become a habit of a lifetime!
- When you first bring your kitten home, show it where the food and water are and then put it on the litter tray. Gradually introduce it to the parts of your home where it will be allowed to go, letting it take its time to become familiar with the household layout. Remember that it will look and smell strange to your kitten and you must do your best to ensure that it feels safe and secure. Until you are sure that it is familiar with everything, it best not leave your kitten on its own.

Settling In – Outdoors

If you are going to allow your kitten to go outside, get it used to wearing a collar as soon as possible. Try not to let your kitten out for at least two or three weeks after you have brought it home; remember also that the inoculations do not have an instant effect and your kitten will still be vulnerable to infection for a week or two.

When you first introduce your kitten to the 'great outdoors', consider the following points.

- For the first few outings, always accompany your kitten.
- Make any dangers safe; for example, cover over fish ponds and swimming pools.
- Secure doors to sheds and out-buildings, especially if they contain chemicals or other preparations that are poisonous to cats.
- Put a 'collar' (see page 117) on any large trees to prevent the kitten climbing higher than is safe for it.
- Watch out for other cats, especially entire toms who may be aggressive towards a young cat.
- Never allow your cat free range until it has established its own territory.
- Never allow a cat out at night.

Meeting Other Family Pets

Cats, especially kittens, are social creatures and usually take to other pets quickly; the resident animal is more likely to feel slightly threatened by the new arrival. Introducing a kitten to an older cat should not be too much of a problem and the two will probably be firm friends in a day or two. If the kitten is unused to dogs, introducing it to one may take longer. Be warned that some breeds of dog are naturally 'ratters' and do not usually accept a cat. While many cats live happily with a rabbit, be very careful to keep other pets, such as mice, rats, hamsters, gerbils, fish and birds, safely away from predatory claws!

- Take plenty of time to introduce the kitten to the resident pet.
- Never leave them alone together until you are quite sure that there is mutual acceptance.
- When you first bring your kitten home, make sure it smells of you. Sprinkle a little of your usual perfume or talcum on a cloth and rub it over the kitten.
- If there is a lot of hissing, try using a 'kitten pen'. The animals can see and smell each other, but the kitten cannot be hurt.
- Always give equal affection to both animals.
- If introducing the kitten to another cat, rub a little sardine or pilchard oil onto their heads and they will soon start to wash each other.
- Feed both cats in the same room and gradually move the bowls closer. They will soon be eating out of the same bowl.

Cats and dogs will usually become firm friends, but do make sure that the initial introductions are well supervised. Never leave them alone together until you are sure they are safe in each other's company.

Kittens and Children

Children can be very persuasive, especially when it comes to what they want for a Christmas or birthday present. Please do not give in if their request is for a kitten. While children usually love kittens, it is not unusual for them to become bored after the initial novelty has worn off and that will usually mean that mother or father is left with the responsibility of the new pet. The decision to introduce a new kitten into your home should be made by the whole family – the kitten will grow into a cat that may well live with you for 18 years or more.

It is important to explain to the children that the kitten is not a toy – it is a small living creature, with feelings and emotions just like humans – and that as it is only a baby, it should be treated like one. It is very tempting to wake the kitten up to play with it, but kittens sleep just as long and soundly as a human baby does. They will also play when they want to!

Always make sure that the kitten is handled properly and gently (see below). It may be tempting for a child to pull the kitten's tail or pick it up by the scruff of its neck, neither of which are good for the kitten.

Always maintain a sensible hygiene regime; if your child is going to be responsible for the new kitten, including cleaning the litter tray, make sure that hands are washed afterwards!

HANDLING CATS AND KITTENS

While a mother cat will carry her young kittens around by the scruff of the neck, humans should never do so, as they could cause injury.

It is often said that 'mother knows best' and this is indeed true of the mother cat – but do not follow her example when handling a kitten or cat. She may well pick her kitten up by the scruff of its neck, but this is not the correct way for humans to handle a young, fragile little creature.

Human contact from a young age is most important for a kitten, as it will help it to become 'socialized'. Equally, it must feel safe and secure.

- Always handle kittens gently.
- Never 'grab' them while they are in a deep sleep.
- Make them feel secure by cradling them in your arms, ensuring that they are well supported at the base of the spine.
- Kittens love to run up your legs, often to sit perching on your shoulder; this may be fun when the kitten is small, but if you do not want 5 kg/11 lb or more of adult cat doing the same, do not encourage such behaviour!
- Adult cats should be treated similarly; always make sure that they are supported from the spine and under their front legs.

When holding a cat,
it is important to
make it feel secure.
Support the back legs
and hind quarters,
cradling it gently in
your arms. Ensure
that your children
are taught to handle
the cat correctly.

2

FEEDING

You are what you eat is a well-known saying and reflects how important diet is to all living creatures, including cats. Food not only provides fuel to keep the body working, it is also the basic source of essential vitamins, minerals and other trace elements that make for a completely balanced diet.

The Importance of Diet

The dental structure of a cat shows that it is a carnivorous animal, but that does not mean that it does not require certain vitamins only to be found in plants. In the wild, a cat catches and devours all of its prey – usually herbivorous or omnivorous animals – and so the cat indirectly receives a nutritional supplement of vegetable matter when it eats the stomach and intestines. The bones provide exercise for the gums and help to keep the teeth clean and healthy.

A huge and lucrative industry has developed out of the need to provide our pets with the correct, properly balanced diet. Expert animal nutritionists have formulated a range of special foods that mimic the diet a cat naturally requires and provide it in 'human-friendly' form in cans, packets, tubs and other containers. For this reason, many people prefer to serve their cats these fuss-free 'convenience foods', as they know that these will provide all the essential nutritional requirements.

Fresh Food

Most cats love fresh food, but it should not be the staple diet unless a complete food is also provided. Many owners cook a fish, poultry or meat meal for their cats to have once a day, relying on the more convenient and scientifically formulated prepared cat foods for the main meal. Some cats like to eat raw meat, but confine this to beef or lamb. Always cook poultry, pork and fish to destroy any harmful bacteria.

Canned Food

This is probably the best-known form of cat food and is available in a huge variety of flavours and textures; even the most discerning cat will find something to suit its palate! These foods usually have quite a high water content, so do not be too concerned if your cat seems to drink little. What they lack is 'crunch' to keep the teeth and gums healthy, so it is advisable to have a bowl of dried food or biscuits available as well.

Dried Food

Within the last decade a wide range of 'hydrolyzed protein' foods have become available. Although they look like cat 'biscuits', they are actually a complete food which many experts recommend as the ideal diet for a cat. They contain all the nutrients a cat requires, as well as providing the all-important 'crunch

factor' to exercise the cat's jaws and help keep the teeth clean. Dried food is extremely convenient to serve, rarely causes stomach disorders and has the added benefit that, unlike fresh and moist foods, it can be left down for a long time without deterioration.

Be especially vigilant about ensuring that a bowl of clean water, preferably bottled mineral water, is always available, as cats fed exclusively on a dried food diet usually need to drink more frequently and a greater quantity than those fed on moist food diets.

Kittens will usually start to show an interest in solid food at about four or five weeks of age and will follow mother's example.

Semi-moist Food

These products are packed in sealed foil pouches and, as there is little moisture, are very clean and convenient to serve. Many cats love them, but do think of them as a treat as they do not always provide the right nutritional balance. They are particularly useful if you take your cat away from home – to cat shows, on holidays and even while the cat is travelling – as they are easy to open, need no preparation and are not messy.

Vacuum-packed Food

This really is the top end of the cat food market – special 'cooked in the container' meals using the best ingredients. As with canned food, they are available in many different 'recipes', but do be warned: some cats may find them far too rich for their digestive systems and may consequently suffer from diarrhoea. They are best used as a treat for special occasions or to tempt the appetite if a cat has gone off its food.

TYPES OF FOOD

Dried biscuits

Semi-moist food

Hydrolized protein food

Canned food

Vacuum-sealed punnet food

Biscuits

Biscuits should not be confused with dried food; although they look similar, the nutritional formulae are quite different and biscuits are not a complete food. They are, however, very useful in hot weather as they do not 'go off' the way that a moist cat food does. It is important that a good supply of fresh water is always available as eating biscuits tends to make cats thirsty and can cause bladder problems in later life. Most cats love them, so use them as a special treat or scatter a few over the top of a moist meal to provide extra texture to the food and valuable stimulation for teeth and gums.

Scraps and Titbits

This is every cat's idea of culinary heaven. If the food is good enough for you, it is certainly going to be of interest to your cat! Habits are not easily broken, so do not start feeding your cat table scraps if this is not going to be a permanent arrangement. Beef and lamb bones are excellent for the teeth, as well as providing nutrition, but avoid pork and poultry bones. Poultry bones, particularly, are likely to splinter and may get stuck in the cat's throat. Although cats are not vegetarians and must *always* have a diet based on meat, they often like vegetables, especially roast potatoes served with a little gravy!

KITTENS – THREE TO NINE MONTHS

If you bought your kitten from a breeder, you will probably have been provided with a 'diet sheet'. This lists the foods the kitten is used to, together with the quantities and times of feeding.

At three months old, a kitten is still very much a baby and requires feeding little and often – three or four small meals a day. There are many specially formulated 'kitten' foods on the market that will help you provide the right balance of nutrition for a growing creature. As the kitten grows older, the meals should become larger and be served less frequently. By the time it is six months old, three meals a day are adequate and at nine months the kitten is considered adult and should be fed only twice a day.

It is important to feed your kitten a variety of different foods. Alternate each meal with a different flavour and texture, using a mixture of canned, dried and fresh foods. If your kitten is used to most types of food, it is less likely to become a faddy eater in later life.

When kittens are first weaned, they will benefit from any of the specially formulated kitten foods, which are available in a variety of flavours and textures.

Hygiene

Cats are clean creatures and do not like eating from dirty dishes. These will also attract flies. Wash them thoroughly after each meal. Do not allow cats to feed from family plates and keep a separate knife, fork and, if appropriate, can opener for preparing the cat's meals.

THE ADULT DIET

From nine months onwards, your cat should be fed twice a day. Once served, fresh, cooked or canned foods will not last very long, especially in hot weather, so do be sure to throw away any food that remains uneaten. For this reason, many owners find the dried hydrolyzed foods more convenient: they contain everything needed for a balanced diet, but can be left out for your cat without any risk of them spoiling.

Unlike dogs, cats do not vary tremendously in size, but some breeds are larger than others and so will require proportionately bigger meals! As a general rule of thumb, a small can of food equates with one meal for one active adult cat.

While dogs can be quite gluttonous creatures, it is less common for a cat to suffer from obesity. Obesity is quite often a result of hormonal problems, such as having been neutered too early. However, some cats are just over-fed (and over-zealous in their eating habits) by over-'caring' owners! Some breeds, such as the British, tend to be less active and can grow to be extremely large if their calorie intake is not correctly monitored. For these reasons many manufacturers have developed a special 'obesity diet' which is particularly suitable for cats in this condition. Consult your veterinarian.

Where and When?

Decide from day one where it is convenient for the food and water bowls to be located. This should be an arrangement that is agreeable to both you and your cat. Unless you want to be constantly tripping up over food bowls, it is

Time-controlled

Glass

usually best to feed your cat on a raised surface. Equally, if you have dogs, very young children or both, they will be unable to reach such a high area and steal your cat's food!

As cats are creatures of habit, it is best to feed them at regular, well-spaced, intervals. This is usually most convenient if it coincides with your own mealtimes – breakfast and supper time for an adult cat. Kittens require an additional 'lunch' and, if less than six months old, an extra tea time or late evening meal.

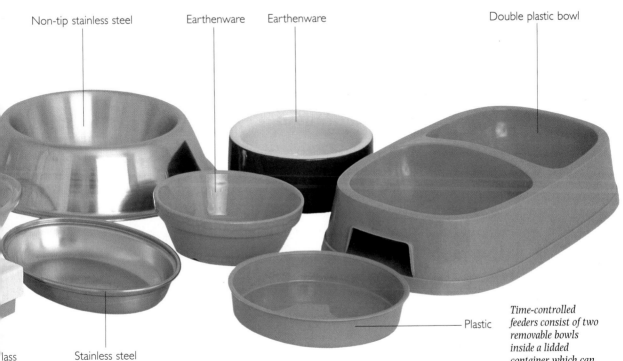

Non-tip stainless steel

Earthenware

Earthenware

Double plastic bowl

Plastic

lass

Stainless steel

Time-controlled feeders consist of two removable bowls inside a lidded container which can be programmed to open at a specific time.
Glass and earthenware dishes can chip or break easily. Earthenware does have the advantage of being heavy and therefore difficult to tip over. Stainless steel bowls cannot easily be damaged and may be sterilized with boiling water if necessary.
Plastic dishes are light and durable.

FUSSY EATERS

Correctly brought up on a well-balanced and varied diet, your cat should not have 'fussy eating' problems. Just like humans, some cats have a preference for fish, meat or poultry; most cats love all of these, but the occasional few do not. As there is now such a wide range of flavours available in commercially produced foods, there should be something that will suit every feline palate.

Warning signs
One word of warning: if your cat is otherwise fit and healthy, but rejects certain types of food, you should consult your veterinarian. It may simply be that your cat is just not 'fishy' or 'beefy' in its tastes, but it could also indicate a digestive problem and so should be investigated. Keep an eye out for problems with teeth and gums, too.

MOTHER CATS

If you are not an experienced breeder of pedigree cats or you own a moggie that has been accidentally mated, then it is really best to consult your veterinarian about any additional foods and/or supplements. If your cat is a pedigree and this is her first litter, the owner of the stud cat may be able to provide advice on a suitable diet during pregnancy. Remember that most veterinarians are not actually cat breeders and sometimes an experienced breeder will be able to give you more detailed, practical information and advice!

It is always sensible to increase the amount of food available while a cat is pregnant, as she has a growing family inside her. Equally, for the first four to five weeks after the kittens are born, until they have been weaned, they will be completely reliant on their mother for nourishment, so her diet should continue to be suitable for both her and the kittens' needs. Many breeders and veterinarians will suggest that the mother cat's diet is supplemented with calcium to promote good, healthy bone development in the kittens, but this should be discussed with the professionals first as it is always possible to overdose on vitamin and mineral supplements .

THE ELDERLY CAT'S DIET

How can one ascertain when a cat is actually 'elderly'? Some cats are 'old' at ten years old or less, while others are extremely fit and active in their teenage years and later!

The most usual problem with an ageing cat is the degeneration of the liver and kidneys; heart problems are also not uncommon. All of these are matters for your veterinarian to deal with and there are many special foods available that will adjust the diet to your cat's particular requirements.

Convenience foods

In general, you will be able to tell when your cat has become 'elderly' as it will be less active than it was in its prime. At this point it is sensible to start using the many convenience, ready-prepared foods that are designed for the 'less active' cat.

MINERALS AND VITAMINS

If you are feeding your cat a proper, well-balanced and varied diet, there should be no need to provide additional vitamins and minerals in the form of supplements. Although you may *think* that you are doing the right thing for your cat, it is quite possible to overdose on these additives and cause your cat to suffer from health disorders.

Cat treats are usually yeast based and are a good source of the B vitamins – but do read the recommended dose on the packet.

Many breeders find that it is useful to give their pregnant queens a calcium supplement, as this promotes strong bone growth in the developing kittens.

It is most important, however, *always to consult your veterinarian before adding any supplements*. Otherwise, you may do more harm than good!

WHAT CATS DRINK

Water is the all-important life giver. Clean, fresh water – preferably bottled, still, mineral water – should always be available to your cat.

Some cats will drink milk, but this is a food more than a drink. Many cats find it too rich and suffer from diarrhoea. Remember that cow's milk is designed for a little calf and not for a much smaller cat or kitten!

Goat's milk is often found to be more suitable and digestible. Recently, specially formulated 'cat milk' has become available from most supermarkets and pet stores.

At a few days old, kittens receive all the nourishment they require and the all-important anti-bodies from their mother's milk. Make sure that you are feeding the mother an adequate, high-quality diet.

3

ROUTINE CARE

You have already given your cat a good start in life by providing it with a sensible, well-balanced and varied diet; now you must think about the regular routine care that your cat will also require. This chapter aims to provide you with helpful advice on all aspects of regular 'feline maintenance'.

Grooming

Cats are fastidiously clean little creatures but, although they will spend a good part of their time involved in both personal and mutual grooming, they can still use a helping hand from their human owner, too. This applies to all cats, not just the pedigrees. The more fur your cat has, the more often it should be groomed; in general, daily for a Persian and at least weekly for a shorthair. Regular grooming not only keeps your cat's coat in pristine condition, it also helps you to:

- detect the presence of fleas or other external parasites and treat them before infestation becomes serious;
- minimize the chances of your cat developing a fur ball;
- notice any sore spots or swollen areas, so that they be treated before they develop into a more serious condition.

Although cats regularly clean their coats, they also require additional grooming, especially if they are longhaired or semi-longhaired, like this Birman.

It is not just pedigree cats that require careful grooming.

Equipment

There is a such huge variety of grooming equipment and accessories on the market that you may find the choice a little bewildering. As with most things, you usually get what you pay for and, as these are items that will be frequently used, you are often better off buying a more expensive product that lasts longer. Metal-toothed combs are one of the most useful items, but do make sure you buy one of really good quality that has rounded, blunt-ended teeth; some of the cheaper ones have sharp teeth that could dig into your cat's skin.

The type of equipment you choose depends on breed, fur length and your preference. If you have bought a pedigree kitten from a breeder, seek his advice, as he will have had much experience of the various products available.

LONGHAIR EQUIPMENT	SHORTHAIR EQUIPMENT
• Bristle brush and wire brush (these can be purchased as a double-sided, all-in-one product) • Wide-toothed comb • Metal comb with alternate long and short teeth • Slicker brush • Toothbrush • Talcum powder	• Bristle brush • Fine-toothed 'flea' comb • Grooming bar • Chamois leather or piece of silk • Bay rum (a natural, aromatic oil)

Use the wide-toothed comb to ease and separate the fur; the long- and short-toothed comb will help to remove any matted areas.

Longhairs

1 Start with the wide toothed comb and gently comb through the coat, paying particular attention to the 'woolly' areas underneath your cat – especially the armpits, tummy and inside the rear legs. These are the areas most prone to matting.

2 Repeat, using the metal comb with alternate long and short teeth.

3 Lightly sprinkle some unperfumed baby powder into the fur, making sure that it does not get into the cat's eyes. This will help the brush to go through the fur more easily, separating each hair and adding bulk to the coat.

4 Using the wire brush, gently and thoroughly brush the coat – gently should be emphasized as it is easy to damage the fur with these brushes. If you do not feel confident using one, skip this part and go on to stage 5. For perfection, brush the coat forwards towards the cat's head, as this will help to 'lift' the fur, adding volume to the final result.

5 Repeat step 4 using the bristle brush.

6 Use the toothbrush to brush the delicate areas of the face.

7 Finally, use the slicker brush; this is not essential, unless you are showing your cat, but will add the 'finishing touch'!

Essential grooming

Regularly grooming a longhaired cat is essential for its well-being, not just its appearance. Otherwise, the fur can quickly become matted, which is not only unsightly but can be detrimental to the cat's health.

Always make sure that the baby powder, used in step 3, is thoroughly brushed out of the coat. If you are showing a pedigree cat, remember that any sign of powder will cause your cat to be disqualified.

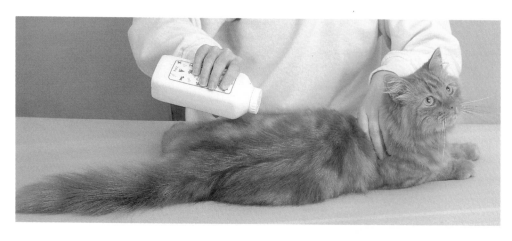

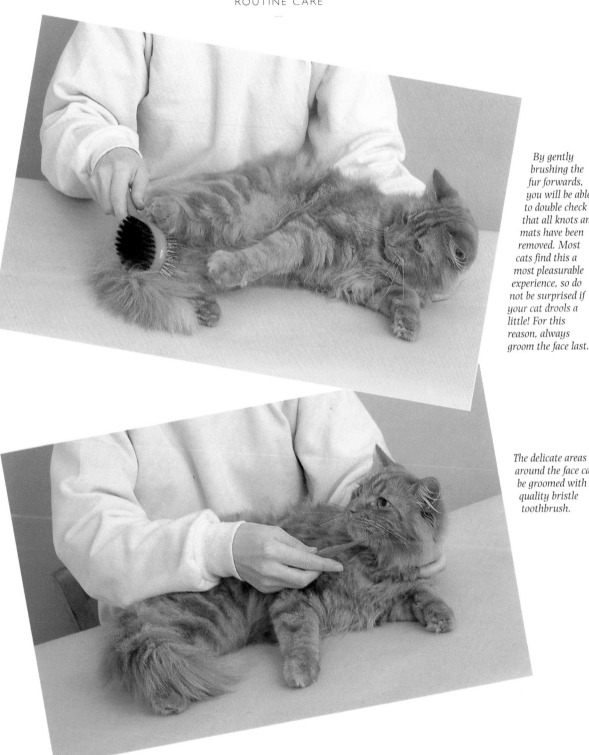

By gently brushing the fur forwards, you will be able to double check that all knots and mats have been removed. Most cats find this a most pleasurable experience, so do not be surprised if your cat drools a little! For this reason, always groom the face last.

The delicate areas around the face can be groomed with a quality bristle toothbrush.

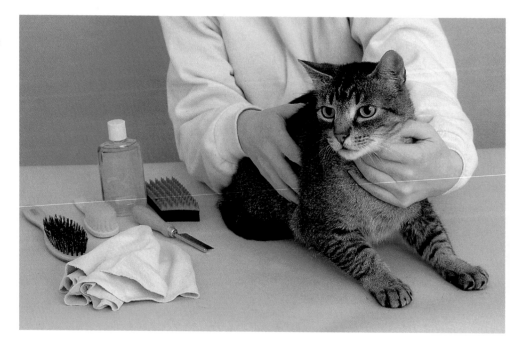

A wide variety of grooming accessories are available. Choose those that best suit your cat's needs.

Shorthairs

Any shorthaired cat will benefit from the use of a grooming bar, which will remove much of the dead fur before combing.

1 Use the grooming bar first; this has little rubber teeth that will loosen and remove excess dead fur.

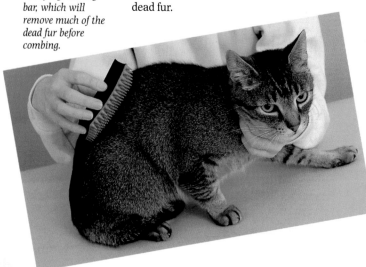

2 Now use the fine-toothed 'flea' comb; this will remove any remaining fur loosened by the grooming bar.

3 Next, using the bristle brush, give the cat a thorough brush.

4 A shorthaired cat will always benefit from lots of 'hand grooming'; this is really just stroking your cat firmly with the palms of your hands, working from the head towards the tail. If your cat is dark coated, sprinkle a little bay rum onto your hands before you start to bring out the colour and shine.

5 Lastly, a polish with a chamois leather or piece of silk will leave the coat smooth and shiny.

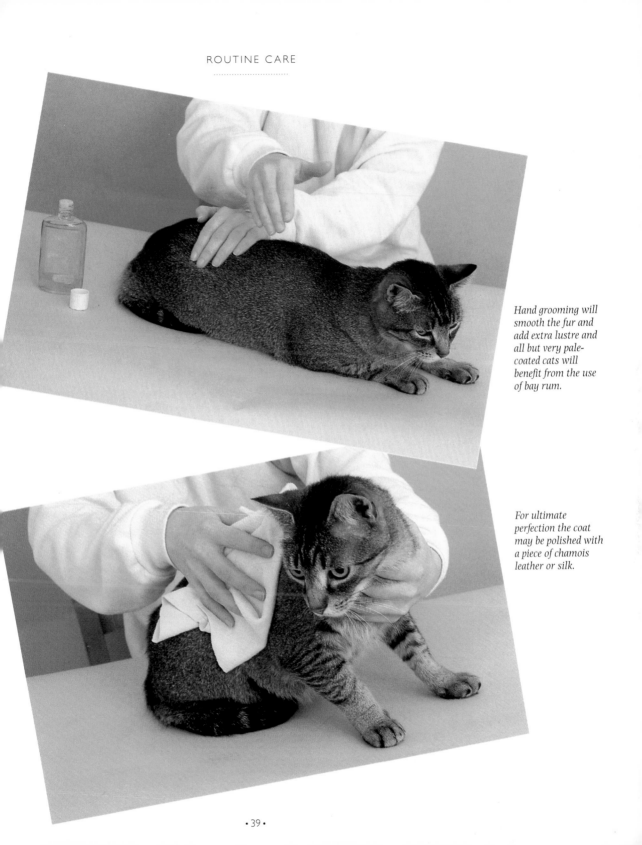

Hand grooming will smooth the fur and add extra lustre and all but very pale-coated cats will benefit from the use of bay rum.

For ultimate perfection the coat may be polished with a piece of chamois leather or silk.

Cleaning delicate areas

The delicate features of your cat (see right) should be inspected as a matter of routine, and cleaned as necessary.

CLEANING EYES, EARS AND TEETH

EYES

A healthy cat should have clear, clean, bright eyes, with no sign of weepiness or discharge. It is not unusual to find a deposit of 'sleep' in the corners of a cat's eyes; this can be easily wiped away with a little damp cotton wool/absorbent cotton, but any persistent discharge should be treated by your veterinarian. Some pedigree breeds have almost 'flat' faces, with very short noses, and this can result in the eyes weeping. Such cats are not ill or infectious but simply have problems with their tear ducts which are unable to drain the tears away.

EARS

When you inspect inside the pinna of your cat's ear, it should look clean. Any waxy deposit can be easily wiped away with a piece of moistened cotton wool/absorbent cotton or cotton bud, but *never* probe into the ear canal, as you could damage this delicate organ. Persistent over-production of wax needs further investigation, as does any sign of dark brown, foul-smelling matter, which usually indicates the presence of ear mites. Both these conditions need veterinary attention.

TEETH

Many cats today are fed on canned foods, which provide little exercise for the gums and teeth. This can cause a build-up of plaque, so a wide range of special 'feline' dental preparations have now been developed. They can be used as toothpaste or plaque inhibitor, and are applied with a 'baby' toothbrush or rubbed on with the finger. These products are available from veterinary practices where they will explain the best way to use them.

CLIPPING YOUR CAT'S CLAWS

Cats that lead an outdoor lifestyle naturally know how to manicure their claws: they scratch them on trees. Indoor cats, unless provided with a scratching post, will use your furniture for the same purpose! Regularly clipping the claws to 'blunt' them will save your furnishings and is quite simple to do once you know how. If you do not know a friend or cat breeder who can show you how it is done, ask your veterinarian to give you a demonstration. These are the basic principles.

• Gently, but firmly squeeze the cats paw to expose the claws.
• Examine the claw; you should be able clearly to see that there is a pink cortex or 'quick' near to the paw. This is living material that contains the blood supply, while the area towards the tip of the claw is white and is composed of dead cells.
• Using nail clippers or special claw clippers, cut off the sharp tip of the claw. Do not cut through the quick, as this will hurt the cat.

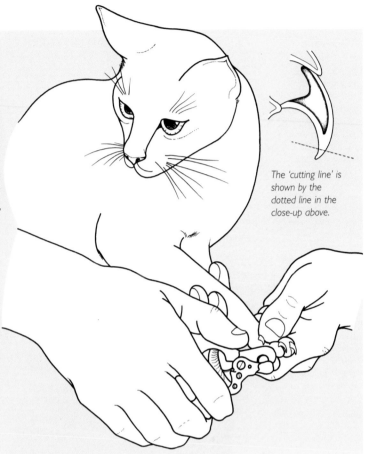

The 'cutting line' is shown by the dotted line in the close-up above.

BATHING A CAT

Cats usually manage to 'wash' themselves quite successfully as they are provided with raspy little tongues exactly for this purpose. Cats should not be washed as a matter of routine, but there are occasions when it may be necessary for you either to wash or 'dry clean' your cat!

Longhaired cats and shorthaired breeds with white or pale coats that are destined for the show bench will benefit from a good wash a few days before the show. Some shorthairs will certainly look better for a 'bran bath' (see page 43), as it removes dirt and other debris from the coat, making it shiny and glossy.

If your cat has been in contact with grease or oil, it will usually have to be bathed to remove these substances. Equally, it might just simply be generally dirty!

Bathing a cat is not that difficult, but you might find it useful to have an extra pair of hands around in case the cat struggles!

Warning

It is not usually necessary to bath a cat unless it has come into contact with grease, oil or toxic substances. Usually cats are bathed only as part of show preparation, especially if they are pale-coated or longhaired. A bath may, however, be needed if the cat has a very severe external parasitic infestation. Do not bath kittens under three months or pregnant queens. Think twice before giving an elderly cat a bath, except on the advice of your veterinarian. Using bran (see opposite), dry shampoo or baby powder may be a better, less traumatic option.

BATHING A CAT WITH WATER

1 Choose a place where that the cat will feel secure and cannot move around too much – the kitchen sink or a baby bath are usually best.

2 Adjust the water to 'hand' temperature.

3 Put the cat in the sink and, using a shower attachment or mixer taps, wet the fur.

4 Apply a little shampoo. Use either a special cat shampoo or one that is safe for babies.

5 Rub in the shampoo well, making sure that you avoid the eyes, and then rinse off.

6 If the coat has any tangles or knots, apply a good quality conditioner and gently comb through. Rinse again.

7 Lift the cat out of the water and wrap in a towel. Towel dry to remove excess moisture.

8 It is important to dry the cat as soon as possible so that it does not catch a chill. In summer, a shorthaired cat will just dry off naturally in the sunshine but, if the weather is cold and the cat does not go outside, a hair drier should be used.

Longhaired cats should always be dried with a hair drier, using stages 3–7 of the grooming instructions.

BATHING A CAT WITH BRAN

1 Put the bran in a bowl and heat in the oven or microwave until it is at 'hand' temperature.

2 Put the cat on a convenient work surface or table in a room that can be easily cleaned – this can be a messy procedure!

3 Rub the warmed bran into the cat's coat, massaging it well into the fur.

4 Remove the bran using a bristle brush.

5 Follow stages 3, 4 and 5 of the grooming instructions.

Natural immunity

Like human babies, kittens obtain immunity from serious infections by absorbing the antibodies present in their mother's milk. From the age of about six weeks, when they are weaned, until 12 weeks, when they may be inoculated, they are at their most vulnerable. It is essential that kittens do not mix with other pets and are confined safely indoors until they have received this vital protection.

INOCULATIONS

To help your cat remain fit and healthy, it should be immunized. There are various infectious diseases with which it may come into contact and your veterinarian will advise you which inoculations are most appropriate. If you have acquired your kitten from a breeder or from a rescue centre, it will normally have received the initial course of injections: you must remember that an annual booster is needed to keep the immunization up to date. Most veterinary practices will remind you, but do make sure that you put the date in your diary, just in case the veterinarian's computer fails!

Do remember that few of these are zoonoses (infections that can be transmitted from cat to human or vice versa).

Cat Flu – Feline Calici Virus (FCV) and Feline Rhinotracheitis (FVR)

While both come under the general term of cat 'flu and affect the upper respiratory tract causing snuffles and sneezes, FCV is a herpes virus that can causes mouth, throat and nose ulcers. A combined vaccine for FIE, FCV and FVR is commonly available and it is *strongly recommended* that this should be used.

Chlamydia

Chlamydia is a distinct organism that presents symptoms similar to cat 'flu. While contagious, it is not particularly common; it is most usually seen in multi-cat households or breeding colonies. Your veterinarian will able to test for it and, if it proves positive, will be able to advise you how best to cope with the situation, as it is possible that even apparently healthy cats within the colony may be carriers of Chlamydia. *A vaccine is available.*

Feline Infectious Enteritis (FIE)

A highly infectious virus which attacks the bowels and central nervous system; it is usually fatal and it is important that *all cats should be inoculated for FIE.*

Feline Immuno-Deficiency Virus (FIV)

This is very similar to FeLV and while experimental vaccines are being tested in the United States and Europe, none are currently available in the U.K.

Inoculation is a quick and completely painless process.

Feline Infectious Leukaemia (FeLV)

This is a virus that affects the cat's natural immune system, making it prone to all manner of other infections. FeLV is usually transmitted by blood and it is apparent that many cats are 'carriers' (i.e. show no sign of illness) but can pass the disease on to other cats. For this reason, many breeders insist on a queen being FeLV negative before they will allow a mating to their stud. It is *strongly recommended* that any cat intended for breeding purposes or who lives a free-range lifestyle where it may get into a fight is immunized.

Feline Infectious Peritonitis (FIP)

Another usually fatal virus which is most commonly seen in the classic 'wet' form, where the cat will display a grossly distended abdomen. The 'dry' form is more difficult to diagnose, as it affects the nervous system. Vaccines are still in the stage of experimental testing, but none are yet licensed for use in the U.K

DEALING WITH PARASITES

External parasites are probably best known in the form of fleas, a problem not just to the cat, but to the whole household if the situation is left untreated and the home becomes infested. The presence of fleas is often indicated if the cat scratches persistently, accompanied by tiny black specks of 'dirt' in the coat – the fleas' faeces which, if brushed out onto a moistened white surface, appear red. Proprietary 'flea collars' are not always effective – indeed the chemicals with which they are impregnated often cause an allergic reaction around the cat's neck. It is always best to consult your veterinarian, who will provide you with a suitable treatment for your cat and, if needed, your house.

Other external parasites are mites and ticks. Ear mites cause a nasty, dark brown, waxy, foul-smelling build-up in the ear, but can be quite easily treated by your veterinarian. Fur mites or 'mange' cause a loss of fur resulting in bald, scaly, scabby patches. As this is easily confused with ringworm, it should be correctly diagnosed and treated by your veterinarian. The tick, like the flea, is a blood sucker. It is often found on farm animals and so is not a common problem to the urban cat. Ticks have hooks on their heads and bury deep under the skin into the flesh, so it is important to make sure that the whole tick is removed or an abscess will develop. They can easily be 'anaesthetized' by applying a swab soaked in surgical spirit. If you do not have this in your first aid box, alcohol, such as gin or vodka, will do just as well! You can then remove the whole tick with a pair of tweezers.

Round worms and tape worms are internal parasites. Both cause the cat to be generally 'off colour': the coat may look out of condition and the stomach is usually enlarged and firm to the touch. There may also be diarrhoea or constipation. Eggs of worms are passed out in the cat's faeces, so wear rubber gloves when changing your cat's litter tray. Tape worm eggs are distinctive in that they resemble grains of rice in appearance. Both types of worms can be treated by a course of tablets that your veterinarian will supply, but routine 'worming' will prevent this becoming a problem.

Rabies (Hydrophobia)

This is a fatal disease which is a zoonosis. As the correct name suggests, the main symptom is a fear of water, but it will cause foaming at the mouth, personality changes and generally 'mad' behaviour. A *vaccine is available* and, as the disease is highly contagious, most countries in which it is endemic insist that *all domestic pets* are immunized.

Household cleaners

Cats are at risk from absorbing toxins through their paw pads as well as by ingestion. Some common household cleaners contain phenols or cresols, both of which are dangerous to cats. Check the labels on disinfectants, kitchen cleaners and antiseptic sprays in particular. Even those which are ostensibly safe may still put your cat at risk if used in too great a concentration. Always follow the manufacturer's instructions for diluting such products.

COMMON HOUSEHOLD HAZARDS

You may think that your house is safe for you and your family, but for an inquisitive cat— think again! There are many normal household items that can endanger a cat's life.

- Washing machines, tumble driers and dishwashers – always double check that your cat is not sitting inside before switching these appliances on.
- Boiling pans – never leave them unattended.
- Electric hobs take time to cool down – if yours does not have a cover, put a pan filled with cold water on the hob.
- Steam from a boiling kettle
- A sink full of hot water
- Bleach, toilet cleaners, detergents, disinfectants and other chemicals
- Thread ties from bin sacks

- Always wrap up chicken, rabbit or other bones that might splinter.
- Sharp knives – especially if they have been used to slice meat
- Toilet – always close the lid, especially if cleaning agents have been used.
- A bath full of hot water
- Electrical and telephone cables – some cats love to chew through them.
- Sewing and knitting materials
- Elastic bands, paper clips, drawing pins, etc.
- Some house plant are poisonous.
- The contents of the garden shed and garage, especially weedkiller, slug poison, lawn fertilizer, anti-freeze, etc.
- Some garden plants and shrubs are poisonous.

Never leave your cat unsupervised in the kitchen. A sink full of water and a slippery, soapy counter could result in a tragic accident.

CATTERIES AND CAT SITTERS

Most people take an annual vacation or more frequent holidays and so their cat/s will have to be left in the care of someone else. This usually means a trip to a boarding cattery but, more recently, new businesses providing a professional 'cat-sitting' service in your own home have become available. There are advantages to both arrangements, but what is most important is that you check out the services that they will be providing for your cat.

Just like hotels, catteries can range from the basic, just tolerable 'pension', providing little more than a bed, food, water and litter tray, to the full 'five star luxury hotel' complete with central heating, comfortable and well-furnished 'chalet', extensive outdoor run with scratching posts, shelves and toys to keep your cat entertained and even the feline cuisine specially prepared to suit your cat's personal palate!

Advertisements can be deceptive, so always go and look at the cattery before letting your cat stay there. Be cautious of those that insist on being available for your inspection only 'by appointment': it might be that

they are genuinely busy, but it could equally be a cover-up for badly run premises that will be given a quick 'spring clean' before you arrive. Most catteries will tell you their opening hours and that you are free to visit within these times.

There is much to recommend the idea of a live-in 'cat-sitter'; not only will your cat feel safe and secure in its own home, but you have the added benefit of knowing, in these times of increasing crime, that your house is being lived in and is thus less likely to be burgled. If you do not know of a friend who has used a cat-sitter who can be recommended, do ask for references and check them out.

Remember that your cat's 'holiday' should be as much of a pleasurable experience as your own holiday would be!

Watch points

• Follow up references given by any professionals to whom you are entrusting your beloved pet and your home.
• Arrange for the cat-sitter to arrive the day before you go away, so that you have time to explain the routine and where everything is kept.
• Always leave a note of where you can be contacted and your veterinarian's name, address and telephone number.

Catteries vary considerably in cost and the facilities they provide.

CARING FOR THE ELDERLY CAT

Reasons for neutering

1 The overriding reason is that there are already far too many unwanted kittens and no true animal lover would want to add to them(see page 20).
2 Spraying, whereby an entire tom marks his territory, is extremely unpleasant and smelly from the human point of view (see page 59).
3 Entire toms are inclined to fight, causing damaged ears and eyes and, possibly, resulting in high veterinary bills.
4 Entire toms are far more likely to stray from home and get lost (see pages 66–67).
5 A calling queen will attract every tom cat from miles around to the detriment of neighbourhood relations.
6 Brothers and sisters will mate with each other with no compunction, so if you have two kittens of different sexes, even if they are never allowed outside, neutering is a wise course of action.

It is difficult to define the word 'elderly' when it comes to cats. Just like humans, some cats become elderly – mentally, physically or both – sooner than others. If you understand your cat well and know its normal habits and behaviour, you will be able to tell when it has reached the 'elderly stage' of its life. Think of your cat rather like a car that has reached the age when it requires a service – your older cat should also have a regular check-up by your veterinarian to make sure it is 'firing on all four cylinders'!

There are some common ailments usually associated with old age that you should watch out for; while some are not curable, most are treatable, enabling your elderly cat to live a happier life. Some veterinarians will advocate the use of alternative remedies (see pages 111–112), as these are generally kinder to the system of an old cat than chemically manufactured drugs and antibiotics. However, as there is a time and a place for both – do take your veterinarian's advice as to what is best for *your* cat. Diet is all-important and information on this can be found on page 32.

These are some common problems associated with old age.

- Arthritis – watch out for any signs of stiffness of joints and/or frequent limping.
- Kidney and liver problems – these can usually be detected by a noticeable increase in thirst.
- Cystitis – the cat will often strain when urinating and the urine produced may be 'spotted' with blood.
- Tumours – regularly feel your cat for unusual lumps; these are usually sebaceous cysts, but should always be investigated.
- Dental problems – keep a check on your cat's teeth and gums; it is not unusual for an older cat to need some extractions.
- Heart attacks and strokes – just like humans, some will recover and others will not; some cats adjust well to their disability and your veterinarian will advise you of how serious the condition is.
- Blindness and deafness – if the cat is otherwise healthy, it is surprising how quickly it can adapt to such disabilities.
- Senility – this is a debatable point as it is not known if cats can suffer from this affliction. However, if your cat gets to the stage when it seems not to know you or where it is and is suffering from incontinence, it may have become senile.

Neutering

Any cat that is not specifically intended for breeding purposes should be neutered, known as altering in the United States. A look around any rescue agency will show just how many unwanted cats are waiting to be re-homed – and no responsible owner would want to add more cats and kittens to the statistics.

The age to neuter a cat is around six months – later, if at all possible, as cats neutered too young may well end up with hormonal problems in adulthood. Some cats and certain breeds are more precocious than others and may display active sexual behaviour at a young age.

There is little that can be done to quieten a young male cat's ardour, but as a female cat

should not be spayed when she is on call, she can be put on a course of the 'feline pill' until she is of a suitable age to have her surgery.

Castration of the male is a relatively simple procedure – some veterinarians joke that it is a bit like shelling peas! The cat is under anaesthetic for a short time and recovers from the ordeal quickly. It is a slightly more serious procedure for a female to be spayed, as it does involve abdominal surgery and takes a little longer. For this reason, the costs of neutering are slightly higher for a female than a male.

Usually, cats are in and out within the day of the surgery and are back to their normal, often boisterous selves the next morning! However, it may take females slightly longer to recover.

Who would guess that this contented family consists of cats aged 15, 16 and 17 years?

4

BREEDING

The decision to breed from your cat should not be taken lightly. It is a tremendous responsibility to bring any new life into the world and, as cats can live to a ripe old age, it is important that you ensure that you will be able to find good, permanent, homes for any kittens.

PROS AND CONS

Ask yourself why you want to breed from your cat. If you have bought a pedigree kitten, you will know the expense involved – and some breeds are far more expensive than others. It does not take a great mathematician to multiply the sale price by five, six, seven or even more kittens and think that breeding from the cat is an easy way to recoup the purchase price and make a hefty profit. Think again: rearing kittens should be done for love, not gain. Just like children, kittens can be very expensive to bring up. The following is a list of are just some of the expenses you are likely to incur.

- You will have to pay a mating fee for the use of the stud cat.
- The stud's owner will usually insist that your queen has a blood test to ensure that she is not carrying any infections.
- Your cat will need more food, care and attention during her pregnancy.

- There may be problems during the pregnancy, kittening and weaning – and veterinary treatment can be expensive.
- The kittens will have to be registered with the Governing Council of the Cat Fancy (GCCF) or other body.
- The kittens will have to be inoculated before leaving for their new homes.

If your non-pedigree cat has just mated with the local tom, you may find that she has contracted one of several sexually transmitted diseases. For this reason, caring owners, who have thought thoroughly before allowing their cat to become pregnant, will often opt to use a pedigree stud cat. Consequently, all the above expenses, apart from the registration fee, will still be incurred with a non-pedigree queen.

It is not always easy to find good homes for pedigree kittens and some breeders will end up with their kittens for several months. It is often even more difficult to place non-pedigree kittens. Before you start, please be sure that you have friends willing to adopt one of your kittens. Rescue centres are often bulging at the seams with them; please do not add to the statistics.

PREGNANCY

About three weeks after your cat has been mated, you will see a visible difference in the colour of her nipples. They will become pinker and this is usually a sure sign that the mating has 'taken'. From now on, she should receive an especially nourishing diet to help her kittens develop strong bones and teeth (see page 32).

Pregnancy usually lasts for 65 days and you should prepare a special box for your cat to have her kittens in. This can be something simple, such as a cardboard box lined with alternate layers of old newspaper and bedding. Kittening can be messy and if you provide her with several layers, it is simple to remove one layer each time a kitten is born, keeping them warm and dry.

The box should be located in a warm, secluded and quiet room, well away from any normal household noise and activity. Introduce your pregnant cat to her 'special place' so that she knows the area and feels safe and secure.

THE ANATOMY OF A PREGNANT CAT

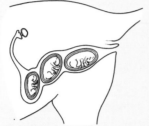

Side view showing the position of the developing kittens in relation to the ovary and fallopian tube.

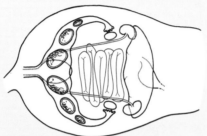

The feline uterus has two 'horns', narrowing towards the ovaries. In large litters, kittens positioned high in the horn may be significantly smaller – the runts of the litter.

Some breeds of cats have larger litters than others. In general, longhairs have smaller litters than the foreign breeds.

Unplanned pregnancy

If your cat's pregnancy was an unplanned accident, you may not be certain when the kittens are due. Indeed, you may even have been unaware of her condition until almost the last minute. Watch out for her nesting procedure; this is a sure sign that the kittens will soon be born.

BIRTH

A few days before the birth is imminent, your cat will start to 'nest'. If she seems discontented with the arrangements you have made for her, you will simply have to bow to her better judgement and move her 'kittening box' elsewhere. Cats are excellent mothers and seem to know exactly what is best for their babies. She may even decide that your bed is the most suitable place for her to give birth! It is important to keep a watchful eye on any queen when she is due to kitten, especially if this is her first litter.

Kittening is usually a simple, straightforward procedure. If you have never seen a cat giving birth before, you will probably be more worried than she is, but most cats know exactly what to do. Remember that cats have multiple births (see page 51) and it is always easier to produce several small babies than one large one!

THE BIRTH PROCESS

- Most cats tend to produce their kittens at night as, in the wild, this would be the safest time for them: be prepared for a long night ahead!
- Once she is comfortably settled, the first sign of impending kittening is that a 'bubble' will appear from her vulva. This is the protective water-filled birth sac containing the first kitten.
- Uterine contractions will become apparent. You will see these as a rippling muscle reflex action, as the mother tries to push the kitten out.
- The 'waters' (that is, the birth sac) will burst and the first kitten should emerge, head first.

- Once the kitten is born, the mother should lick it all over to stimulate its circulation and to dry it off.
- She should also chew through the umbilical cord, releasing the kitten from the placenta. There will be a separate placenta for each kitten, except in the case of identical twins.
- Most cats will then eat the placenta as it provides additional nutrients, but don't be concerned if she doesn't eat them all, especially if it is a large litter.
- The birth will continue in this way until all the kittens are born. They may all arrive within a few minutes of each other, but some cats may take several hours in labour.
- Sit back and enjoy your new feline family!

EQUIPMENT TO KEEP HANDY

- Sterilized blunt-tipped scissors – in case you have to cut the cord
- Clean towels (or kitchen paper towels) – to stimulate the kittens and dry them; sometimes kittens come in a quite rapid

succession and the mother does not have time to clean them all up.
- Telephone – in case you need to call the veterinarian. Keep his or her telephone number to hand, too.

PROBLEMS DURING BREEDING AND KITTENING

You should inform your veterinarian of your cat's pregnancy and he may suggest regular 'ante-natal' check-ups.

Although your cat may have been mated, it is possible that she may:
• have a 'phantom' pregnancy
• re-absorb some or all of her kittens early in pregnancy.

More serious conditions that may occur during kittening and later will require urgent veterinary attention.
• Uterine inertia – this is when a cat's muscles can no longer contract during kittening. Your vet will be able to administer an injection to stimulate her back into labour, but if this does not work, a Caesarean section may be necessary.
• Always make sure that a placenta is expelled with each kitten – any retained will cause an infection.

• A kitten may become stuck in the birth canal. This can often be 'manipulated' and pulled out with clean, well-lubricated fingers, but do not try to do this if you have never done it before.
• Metritis– this is a uterine infection more commonly seen in cats that have recently given birth.
• Mastitis – if the mammary glands become infected, they will usually feel hot and lumpy to the touch. Not only will the mother cat feel unwell but, if the kittens are still suckling, they may well suffer from her poisoned milk.
• Loss of milk – this may be caused by mastitis, but also results from other causes. Whatever the cause, you will have to foster-feed the kittens with a special feeding bottle until they can be weaned onto solid foods.

Your veterinarian will advise you of the most suitable liquid formula to use until the weaning process starts.

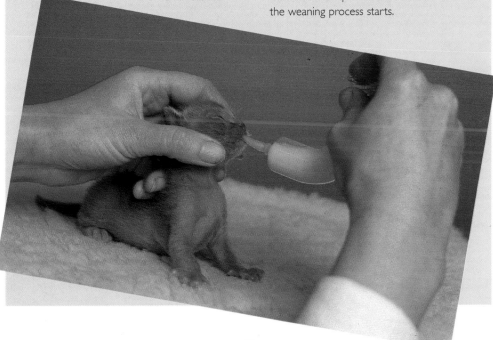

If a kitten is orphaned or the mother is unable to feed it, you will have to foster feed it with a special bottle and milk formula every few hours throughout the day and night.

Kittens are born blind and helpless and are completely dependent on their mother.

NEWBORN KITTENS

After the kittens are born, make sure that the mother cat is happily settled with her new family. Although they are born blind, the kittens usually have no difficulty in locating a nipple with a gentle nudge from their mother, but make sure that each kitten is 'plugged' in. As the mother should have eaten at least one of the highly nutritious placentas, she will probably not be hungry. However, a little white fish or a chicken meal may be appreciated. Once you are confident that she and her family are content and settled, leave them to sleep.

The mother cat usually provides for all the kittens' needs until they are three or four weeks old. She will supply all the required nourishment and keep them and their nest clean and warm.

GROWING KITTENS

Kittens are born with their eyes closed and should be left safe in their kittening box in the quiet, darkened room in which they were born. Keep a check on their progress and ensure that they are all suckling well. Let the kittens become accustomed to your sound, smell and touch; human contact at an early age will help them to become socialized. However, limit the number of human visitors to you and maybe one other member of the family and please do not invite all the neighbours in to play with the kittens until they are quite a lot older!

The kittens' eyes will start to open when they are about ten days old. By two weeks old they will be quite actively moving around their box. By the time they are three weeks old they will start to climb out of their box and explore their new world. At this point, you might find a kitten pen handy. It will keep the kittens safely confined, especially from the dangers of large human feet.

Feeding Time

The kittens will be ready for solid food (see page 56) from about four weeks onwards. At this point they will also require a litter tray. Some kittens are a little confused between food and

From four weeks old the kittens will start exploring and begin to venture away from the safety of their mother and the nest.

Careful planning

If you have decided to breed from your cat, plan well in advance. Do not have your kittens ready for sale during the summer holiday period, when kittens are difficult to place, or at Christmas when they may be bought on a whim as a present.

litter and may try to eat the latter. A simple tip is to put a little urine-soiled litter in their tray at first. They will soon realize that this is not for eating! The mother cat will wash their abdomens vigorously after they have eaten, stimulating their bowels and bladders to 'perform'. She will then pick them up and gently put them on their tray. Kittens do not usually have to be 'litter trained' by humans, as their mother will teach them all they have to know about toilet habits. Quite soon, they will be following mother's example and learn very quickly. Your job is simply to ensure the litter is changed regularly.

Weaning the Kittens

From now until the kittens are ready to leave home, you will have your hands full. The kittens will require weaning; some take to this quite easily, but others are lazy and find a quick suck from the milk bar much easier. If any are reluctant to eat, try them on a *very* small quantity of strongly smelling foods, such as canned sardines or pilchards in tomato sauce. These are far too rich as a basic diet for such a young animal but, for some reason, cats seem to love them. Once they are all used to eating, follow the simple guidelines set out on page 29.

FINDING HOMES FOR THE KITTENS

This is the heart-breaking time when your little family has to leave you and their mother. Do not delay finding suitable homes until the kittens are ready to leave you, but plan properly in advance:

• Let your friends know when your cat has had kittens and that you will be seeking homes for them in three months' time.
• If your cat is a pedigree, let the breed club secretary know, so that they may be registered on the 'kitten list'.
• Advertise in the 'cat' press and your local newspaper.
• Ask your veterinarian if you can put a card on his notice board.

These will probably bring you lots of inquiries; now you have to interview the prospective owners to be sure that they are really going to give your precious kittens a *permanent*, loving home that matches your standards.

• Be wary of people who ask 'are they good ratters and mousers?' – this usually means that they are not looking for a pet and that your kitten will be left to fend for itself.
• Always ask what their working arrangements are and if the kitten will be left on its own for most of the day. If they have no other pets, encourage them to take two kittens as company for each other.
• Ask if they have a dog and, if so, which breed. Some breeds are natural ratters and they will often attack a cat, too.
• Ask if they have children and, if so, what age. If the children are very young and have never owned a cat before, it may be better for them to wait until they are older and ready to accept the responsibility of pet ownership
• If your kittens are pedigree, ask if they have any intention of breeding; there are some unscrupulous 'kitten farms' around and you

The Learning Curve

The kittens will start learning to play and will take a lively interest in all that is going on in your home. Provide them with plenty of toys and stimulating activities to keep their bodies and minds alert. They should become acquainted with the normal household activities, especially the use of noisy appliances, such as televisions, radios, vacuum cleaners and washing machines. However, do keep an eye out that they do not get themselves into any life-threatening situations. Young kittens are just as inquisitive as young children and can get into just as much mischief – you really will need eyes in the back of your head!

Leaving Home

By the time the kittens are 12 weeks old and ready to leave home, they should be fit, healthy, active little creatures that are well socialized towards humans and used to most things that the average home has to offer. They should also be fully inoculated, wormed and registered if a pedigree breed. You should also provide the new owners with a diet sheet, so that they will know what the kitten has been used to eating.

Avoiding further pregnancies

Once the kittens have been weaned, the queen can quickly become pregnant again. Even if one or two kittens are still suckling occasionally, pregnancy may still occur, although it is less likely. If this litter was unplanned, now is the time to discuss spaying with your veterinarian and to make an appointment.

would not want one of your kittens to end up there. You can have your kittens put on the inactive register (where they may not be shown or bred from) or over stamped 'not for breeding'.

- Never sell the whole litter to one buyer. This usually means that they will be destined for some disreputable place, such as a research laboratory.

You will probably find that you will have a 'gut reaction' if any of the would-be purchasers seems unsuitable; just be very firm and say 'No!' Always tell the new owners that they should contact you if their kittens are not settling in well or if they have any problems. Do make a point of 'following up' the kittens' progress for the first few weeks and make sure you keep a record of addresses.

Finally, if, for any reason, the cat has to be re-homed in later life, you must be prepared to take the responsibility. After all, it was your decision to have kittens in the first place, not your cat's.

Advise prospective owners of the size and personality they can expect when the kitten grows up. This cute little bundle of fluff is a Maine Coon, which will grow up to be one of the larger varieties of cat.

5

THE SOCIAL CAT

While it is quite possible to 'educate' a child, 'cajoling' is a better term to use when dealing with the fickle cat! Get to know your cat and, with a little gentle persuasion, it might just agree with your way of thinking! Several books have been written about training cats – sadly, none of them by cats. As they do seem to be the most self-opinionated creatures, given half the chance, they would probably write a magnificent tome on how they would like to live.

Cat owners usually wish to share their homes with these creatures not only because of the cat's independent nature, but also because it is the nearest most people will ever come to living with a small example of a wild animal. They would not wish to live with a pet that could be 'trained' to obey like a dog, but do expect it to behave with some decorum within a domestic environment.

Educating your Cat

Your cat will, if allowed, rule your household, so all 'house rules' should be made clear from the start. Make it quite plain which areas of your house your cat is allowed into and what it may or may not do. If you are taking in a new kitten, this is quite easy to do. Just be very firm when the kitten does something that you do not want it to do and say 'No' in an authoritative voice; the kitten will quickly learn that it is displeasing you. This process will usually take longer if you are adopting an older cat with an already established behaviour pattern. It is a matter of perseverance, but your cat will respect you all the more if you make sure that it realizes that you are the one who is 'top cat' and the one who should be 'obeyed'.

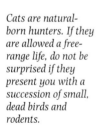
Cats are natural-born hunters. If they are allowed a free-range life, do not be surprised if they present you with a succession of small, dead birds and rodents.

ANTI-SOCIAL HABITS

Many of these anti-social activities are caused by deep-seated behavioural problems, they often respond well to homeopathic or herbal remedies. Always contact your veterinarian for a correct diagnosis of the clinical condition.

Spraying

This is usually associated with an entire tom cat wanting to mark its territory. This is fine if your cat confines this activity to the garden, but it becomes a problem when the cat sprays indoors, as the smell is horrendous. Certain breeds – male or female (especially a female on call), neutered or not – and cats that live in overcrowded conditions may also spray. The tell-tale sign of spraying is when the cat puts its tail into an upright position and 'twitches' it. Neutering is the obvious answer but, if the cat is already neutered, your veterinarian may recommend a course of treatment.

'Peeing and Pooping'

Performing these activities in the wrong place should not be confused with spraying. This behaviour may occur if you do not provide your cat/s with a regularly cleaned litter tray. In an older cat, it could indicate kidney or liver infection. In a younger cat, it is quite often caused by insecurity.

Aggression, Fighting and Biting

If this is directed towards other cats in the household, it is usually because of over-crowding. It is tempting to keep several cats, but some breeds will not tolerate a multi-cat household. This can be cured by reducing the number of cats you own.

If the aggression is aimed towards you and your family, there may be a good reason:

perhaps a child has handled the cat badly. Some cats give 'love bites' as a way of showing affection; this can be painful, as they usually nip you on the cheek or ear, but it is your cat's way of saying that it loves you!

If a cat is persistently aggressive towards you, seek professional help.

Chewing Wool, Cotton and Other Fabrics

This may be a behavioural problem, a little like a child's need to suck its 'comfort and security' blanket. It can also indicate that the cat's diet is lacking in fibre and you may need to change its normal feeding regime.

Clumsiness

Just like people, some cats are clumsier than others. You cannot 'cure' this, but if you have valuable ornaments, it is best to keep them securely out of the cat's way!

Scratching

Cats have a natural way of providing themselves with a manicure: they like to preen their claws! In the wild this is performed on a tree or other natural object. If you do not provide your cat with a suitable cat scratching post, expect your furniture to suffer the consequences.

Think 'cat'

Cats often do things that may be quite natural to them, but are really rather anti-social to any humans with whom they live. There are often good reasons for such behaviour. There are now even clinics that have been set up with special 'animal behaviourist' practitioners; some even describe themselves as 'cat shrinks'! However, many of these problems can be sorted out quite easily if you *understand* your cat and why it is behaving in such a manner.

Your cat may have to fight to establish its territorial rights, which may result in battle scars.

Catnip

Your cat is quite likely to go 'wild' for a toy stuffed with this dried herb, pouncing and tossing it about and even drooling with sheer ecstasy.

Life is one long game for a kitten and it will find innumerable ways to amuse itself. This looks like harmless fun, but this little girl could have got herself tangled in the handles of this old shopping bag if her owner had not been watching.

Playing

What could be more delightful than watching a mother cat playing with her kittens or, indeed, a grown-up cat amusing itself with a toy mouse or a piece of string? Many cat owners will say that they prefer watching the antics of their cats to switching on the television!

Do not be fooled into thinking that cats perform simply for our entertainment. 'Play' provides a much more serious function related to their survival in the wild. As soon as kittens are able to walk, a mother cat will encourage them to pounce on and play with her tail. This is an endearing sight to us, but has a quite different purpose from the mother cat's point of view. She is teaching her kittens the first principles of hunting prey. The kittens concentrate on every twitch of her tail and pounce at just the right moment, as if catching something that would provide them

with a valuable meal. She is also teaching them to make use of two of their most valuable assets – agility and claws.

Unlike puppies, kittens are almost fully co-ordinated as young as five weeks old and for good reason. Dogs are 'pack' hunters and, in the wild, the adults will always feed and protect the younger members of the pack until they are fully mature. This is not the case with cats. Most feline species tend to hunt alone and will expect their kittens to be able to fend for themselves and be self-sufficient at a much younger age. It is important that a mother cat teaches her kittens all the 'tricks of the trade' as soon as possible as, without such knowledge, they would have little chance of survival.

The modern pet cat has no need to use these inherited hunting traits. Cats have their (human) slaves to provide them with food, water and every creature comfort they could desire, including an abundance of toys to 'play' with. So why do we still give them toys? Certainly they provide us with the amusing sight of our pets stalking, leaping, jumping, pouncing and retrieving but, if we are honest, it is the fact that we like the idea of having a domesticated wild animal sharing our home! We feed and water them and tend to their every need, so it is not surprising that most cats seem to walk around with a smug smile on their faces. They know full well that we need them more than they need us. By providing them with toys, we are helping them to exercise their natural instinct to hunt and kill.

The agility, grace, dexterity and strength of cats is never more apparent than when they are playing.

Warning

It is sensible to remove anything detachable from cat toys, such as pieces of elastic, the 'eyes' of a catnip mouse or a bell that is not fully enclosed. Cats take their play seriously and claws and teeth will soon remove these items if you do not, resulting in a choking kitten or some other kind of accidental injury.

Eating grass

Cats use grass as a natural emetic; it clears out their stomachs and makes them sick. If they live indoors and do not have any grass to chew, they will eat what they can find – often to the detriment of your favourite houseplants (some of which are poisonous). You can buy specially prepared 'cat grass' in small tubs; this can easily be grown on a sunny window sill.

This cat could have gone in and out at will when its owners were at work if they had fitted a cat flap.

Cats Outdoors

Cats are territorial creatures and, afforded access to the great outdoors, will soon establish their own local territory. While this is the most natural way for a cat to live, there are many dangers out there, especially in an urban area. We, their owners, must be responsible for any injuries resulting from cat fights and other accidents, not to mention the often heavy veterinary fees that might be incurred.

Any cat that is allowed to wander freely should carry some form of identification. A collar, with an elasticized strip to help the cat escape if the collar becomes hooked on a branch or some other object, should bear a tag with the name and address of the owner. It is also advisable to mark the inside of the collar (in indelible ink with the house number and post or zip code).

Many veterinarians now recommend micro-chipping or tattooing. These simple procedures can be performed when your cat is under anaesthetic, preferably while it is undergoing necessary surgery, such as being neutered. However, if your cat is destined for the show bench, a tattoo is considered a 'distinguishing mark' in the U.K. and the cat will be disqualified.

You can buy special 'houses' for cats, with outside runs attached. Many owners find that this is a quite acceptable way to allow their cats the best of both worlds. You could also build a specially constructed run with direct access from a cat flap or kitchen window, so that it looks less intrusive. Tree stumps, shelving and ladders will afford your cats hours of amusement if you are at work and the cats will benefit from the fresh air.

Even better, if your garden is not too large, is to 'cat proof' it with wire mesh or a similar material because this allows a high degree of natural freedom combined with the greatest level of protection from traffic and other creatures that may be dangerous to cats. This need not be prohibitively expensive and the offending wire can always be covered with climbing plants – do be sure that the plants you select are not poisonous to cats.

If none of these is possible, then you can train your cat to a harness and lead; you will be able to walk your cat in the garden in the full knowledge that you can keep it safe and sound. Many breeds take happily to this idea, but do be careful if you venture outside known territory, such as to the local park, as your vulnerable cat might be attacked by a dog.

Cats love to climb and a tree collar (see page 117) will prevent them climbing higher than is safe.

Cats are perfect companions to people of all ages and will take a lively interest in sharing your hobbies.

CATS AND PEOPLE

Whether young or old, we can all benefit from owning a 'companion animal', or pet, and the cat is one of the most responsive and affectionate and one of the least demanding. What is important is to choose one that will fit into your particular lifestyle.

As a general rule of thumb, age is the deciding factor. An older cat may not enjoy the noise and activity of a family with young children. Equally, an energetic young kitten may not be suitable for an older, less active, person.

Young animals and young humans usually work well together. A kitten may be small, but nature has provided it with sharp claws and teeth. If a child is rough with it, the kitten will react to protect itself. On the other hand, if the kitten is treated with care and respect, the child will soon develop a friendship with it that is based on a mutual trust.

At the other end of the scale, the benefit of 'companion animal' ownership for the elderly is well documented. Cats are particularly suitable as, unlike dogs, they do not need to be taken for regular and often lengthy walks – something that many elderly people would be incapable of doing. However, they still need a certain amount of attention and will keep you active! A cat will make you get up in the morning to feed it, it will keep you amused when you play with it and, most importantly, it will purr. The cat has been jokingly called 'a small furry tranquilliser on four paws' – an apt description. The medical profession widely acknowledges the therapeutic effect of living with a cat. The calming effect of

A child and a kitten growing up together will share many years of close friendship and lasting affection.

stroking a purring cat is thought to reduce the chances of a heart attack.

Many cats live with the average '2.4 children' family and it is important to make the ground rules from day one. Will the cat be allowed to sleep on – or in – the beds? It is tempting to allow a new feline arrival to share your bed 'just for the first few nights', but from the cat's point of view this is now the correct place for it to sleep and it will not be pleased to find itself suddenly banished to a cat basket elsewhere. Is it allowed on the dining table and kitchen counters? It may be tempting to let your cat have a few titbits from the table 'just to settle it in and to make it feel like part of the family', but the cat will expect this to be the norm at mealtimes.

Habits are hard to break and, despite the common misconception that cats 'cannot be trained', they do respond to discipline. In the wild, there is always a 'top cat'; in a domestic environment, this is not always the case as many cats live without feline companionship. Make sure that your cat knows that you are the top cat and you should live in mutual harmony for many years to come!

Stealing food

Given the opportunity, any cat will *want* to steal a tasty morsel from your plate. However, if it has been properly educated from the outset, it will know when and where it may eat.

If you adopt a feral cat, realize that it is not completely self-sufficient and will rely on you for at least one meal a day. It is a fallacy that cats hunt better on an empty stomach! You must also be prepared to be responsible for their veterinary needs.

STRAYS AND FERALS

The term feral was applied to stray domestic cats that had reverted to their natural wild cat ways. They were usually abandoned, unwanted pets that had bred indiscriminately and had to fight for survival. In the western world today, most people have been educated towards the idea of responsible pet ownership and so this problem does not arise in the first or second generation of abandoned cats. Modern ferals are usually several generations away from a knowledge of a domestic environment and often cannot be

FINDING A MISSING CAT

- Search your home thoroughly. Although you think your cat has gone missing, it is quite likely that it is still safely indoors and asleep in a drawer, cupboard, cardboard box, airing cupboard or other suitably feline-friendly place.
- Check all garages, sheds and out-buildings and ask your immediate neighbours to do the same.
- Contact local veterinary practices, cat rescue organizations, cat clubs and, if a pedigree, the breed club as most will run a 'lost and found' register. Also notify the local police station. (While they do not strictly deal with lost cats, if you mention the cat is a valuable pedigree that may have been stolen, it has to be construed as possible theft.)

- Make a notice, with a good description of your cat, advertising that it is lost. Incorporate a photograph, if possible. It is worth keeping one detail about the cat to yourself so that you can check that callers claiming to have found it really are genuine, not cruel hoaxers. Deliver the notices to the neighbourhood houses and ask the local shops to display one in their windows. (It is a wise precaution not to include too many personal details about yourself.)
- Tell the newspaper boy, postman and any other delivery men who are up early in the morning; cats revert to a 'feral' existence quite quickly and are more likely to be spotted by an early riser.
- If you live near a school, ask the

handled, as they are unused to human contact or are justifiably nervous if they have suffered cruel treatment. They are often found in colonies sharing warmth, shelter and food. In towns this is likely to be in such places as warehouses, factories and hospitals; in the country, they are usually what are termed 'farm cats'.

These cats are often considered the pariahs of polite society, especially in the grander areas of a city. They are often scruffy, battle-scarred and, if they have not been neutered, noisy when they are performing their mating rituals. Fortunately, there is a growing trend to look after these poor cats and many charities are concerned solely with their welfare. They trap and neuter them where possible. They are then returned to their natural colony, regularly fed and monitored for health problems. If the cats cannot be caught for neutering, their food will be laced with a feline contraceptive to inhibit a population explosion. It is sometimes possible to re-home ferals, but as they will have spent so much time living 'rough', it is often kinder to relocate in the country where they will be able to lead a more natural life. As an added bonus they will help control garden vermin, such as rabbits, rats and mice.

headteacher or principal to announce your missing cat at assembly. Many children have pets of their own and, because they appreciate the upset caused by a lost cat, will keep an eye out for yours.

• While offering a reward might seem a good idea, do be careful: it might actually encourage someone to steal a cat for monetary gain.

• If you have another cat, take it out in a secure carrier on a night-time patrol; it will most probably meow and, if its companion is locked in somewhere, you will be quite likely to hear its voice answering.

• Check your local area for any empty premises, especially those which are being renovated. It is possible your cat has wandered in and become locked in or otherwise stranded by accident.

• Contact the local cleansing department responsible for street cleaning; they have to report any animals found run over. You might find it less traumatic to ask a friend to make this telephone call for you, but it is better to know than not.

• Never give up hope: cats are notorious for getting into strange cars and other vehicles and yours may well be several hundred miles away. Once its loss has got into the 'missing cat' network, you may well get it back, even after several months.

When your cat has been found, safely or otherwise, always notify all the people you have contacted. Many of them will have spent time and effort trying to locate your pet, often at their own expense.

Prevention is better than cure

It cannot be stressed enough that if your cat is allowed outside, it should have clear identification.
• A collar with a name tag giving *your* name, house number post/zip code and telephone number.
• Tags do fall off, so write the same information inside the collar with indelible ink.
• As cats may also lose their collars or have them removed maliciously, many veterinarians recommend the use of the Identichip. If your cat should wander off, these will help speed its safe return.

6

A GALLERY OF BREEDS

Longhair (Persian)

• Exotic Shorthair

Semi-Longhair

• Birman
• Maine Coon
• Norwegian Forest Cat
• Ragdoll
• Somali
• Turkish Van

British Shorthair

• Manx

Foreign

• Abyssinian
• Bengal
• Burmilla – Asian group
• Cornish Rex
• Devon Rex
• Japanese Bobtail
• Korat
• Ocicat
• Russian Blue
• Singapura
• Sphynx
• Tonkinese

Oriental

• Angora

Burmese

Siamese

• Balinese

Pedigree cats come in a bewildering array of shapes, sizes, colours, patterns and fur length, but do not be swayed by looks alone; beneath each furry (or, in some cases, 'furrily' challenged!) exterior is a quite individual personality, some more demanding than others. This gallery will give you a fair idea of what to expect and you can see examples of recognized breeds at any all-breed show.

CHARACTERISTICS AND PERSONALITIES

Longhaired or Persian cats are generally 'laid back' and relatively undemanding, apart from the regular daily grooming required to keep their coats free from knots. The British Shorthairs have a similar attitude ('the next best thing to a fireside moggie', as one breeder describes them). In general, neither of these breeds is particularly energetic or athletic.

At the other end of the scale, there are Burmese, Orientals and Siamese. Given half the chance, these breeds would be working out at the gym every day, preparing themselves for the next Olympic Games – and they expect their owners to share their activities with them.

The six breeds classified within the Semi-Longhair section – Birman, Maine Coon, Norwegian Forest Cat, Ragdoll, Somali and

Turkish Van – are more outgoing in personality than the Persian Longhairs, but not usually quite so demonstrative (or noisy) as the Burmese, Siamese and Orientals. Although their fine silky coats do not mat easily, these breeds still require regular grooming.

The Foreign section contains a multitude of differing breeds; old favourites, such as the Abyssinian with its 'wild cat' ticked coat, the elegant Russian Blue, the Korat, another blue-only variety, the pixie-like and mischievous Devon Rex and the similarly curly-coated Cornish Rex, as well as newer varieties, such as the Burmillas and Tonkinese. More recent imports, which are currently unrecognized by the Governing Council of the Cat Fancy (see below), include the Sphynx, Singapura, Bengal, Japanese Bobtail and Ocicat.

CAT FANCIES

'Cat Fancies', the proper term for the governing bodies that register and supervise the breeding of pedigree cats, exist in many countries. The 'Standard of Points' sometimes vary, as do the groups to which the cats are allocated. For the purposes of this book, the breeds are described to the standards laid down by the original, British Fancy, the Governing Council of the Cat Fancy and are loosely classified within the seven sections that the G.C.C.F. registration system and shows are organized by.

Cats are, in general, judged on type (the physical bone structure). Wherever an existing breed of shorthair has a semi-longhair equivalent, it will be found in the shorthair group (with the exception of the Somali). Equally, those unrecognized breeds have been placed in the section to which they are most likely to be allocated.

CHOOSING YOUR BREED

Before you make a decision on a particular breed, go and visit them 'in the fur' in a domestic situation. Your cat may well live to be 18 years or more and you need to be sure that you and your cat are going to be compatible. A home visit will tell you far more about the breed's personality and behaviour than any amount of words and pretty pictures!

Of the pedigree groups, Burmese are among the most popular.

Longhair (Persian) Breed

The Persian, or longhair, is a most popular breed of cat. They are generally very sweet-natured, even-tempered and not too demanding of your attention.

●

With their long, luxuriant fur, Persians are a truly glamourous breed and are available in such a wide range of coat colours and patterns that there should be a variety that appeals to even the most discerning of aesthetes. However, remember for all the 'plus' points, you must dedicate ten minutes or so a day to the maintenance of their coats.

PROS AND CONS

Plus Points	Minus Points
• Relatively undemanding	• Need regular, daily grooming
• Quiet voices	• Long fur will show up more on your furnishings and carpets
• Loving and sweet-natured	
• When adult, not usually overly active	• Not so active as some breeds
	• Can be faddy eaters
• Do not mind sharing their home with several other cats	
• Will not constantly pester you for games and attention	
• Good with children	
• Often happy to be a sole cat	

This Self Black kitten shows a great deal of promise for the show bench, as it conforms to all the correct standards.

A more recent trend is to breed Persians of the 'ultra' type, which are similar to, but less extreme than, the Peke-faced in the United States. This is an Orange-Eyed, White 'ultra' Persian.

The Colourpoint, known as the Himalayan in the United States, is one of the 'man-made' colours and one that is extremely popular. This Cream Point is a Supreme Grand Champion, the highest of accolades.

The Exotic Shorthair is a cat of true Persian type, but without the luxuriant coat and so is ideal for people who like the appearance of Persians but cannot cope with the grooming.

Smokes are one of the oldest of Persian colours and have tended to go in and out of fashion. They are currently rather popular.

Semi-Longhair Breeds

This section covers several breeds, all with very distinctive and different looks, but with certain similarities in character and temperament. In general, they need less grooming than the Persian as their silkier coats are less likely to knot and mat.

●

They are more outgoing and adventurous in attitude, but not so boisterous and noisy as the Foreigns, Burmese, Siamese and Orientals.

●

Allowing for your own personal preference for shape and size, there is really little in the way of bad points: they are highly companionable and make good family pets.

●

PROS AND CONS

Plus Points	Minus Points
• Friendly and intelligent	• Do not like to be left alone
• Need only a limited amount of extra grooming	• Need some extra grooming
• Glamourous looks	
• Outgoing, active and playful	
• Good with children and other animals	

*The Birman is
probably the most
popular of all the
breeds found in this
section. This Cream
Point is one of the
newer colours.*

The Birman is also known as the 'sacred cat of Burma', highly-prized by the Buddhist monks and sacred to their temples. This Grand Premier Seal Point is an example of the original colour pattern.

From eastern Turkey comes the Turkish Van, an unusual breed in that it loves to swim in water.

From across the Atlantic comes that 'Yankee cat' – the Maine Coon – one of the largest breeds. It is becoming increasingly popular in the U.K. This Red Tabby is a fine example.

The Norwegian Forest Cat is a hardy breed with a thick coat, but is also noted for its grace and dexterity. It is thought to be the descendant of the 'fairy' cat referred to in Norse legends. It is regularly seen gracing the show benches in both Europe and the United States.

Another breed developed in the United States is the Ragdoll. It is renowned for its gentle nature. Another of the larger breeds of cat, this Seal Colourpointed is a splendid specimen.

Recently moved from the Foreign group, the Somali is the Semi-Longhair equivalent of the Abyssinian and displays a typical 'foxy' ruff and brush-like tail.

British Shorthair Breed

These are the 'gentle giants' of the cat world: easy going, even-tempered and sweet-natured. They like nothing better than to curl up in a warm place and sleep!

●

They are solid, chunky-looking cats, similar in personality to the Persian and are available in just as many coat colours and patterns.

●

While some of the newer colours and patterns have been genetically engineered, the breed in general is thought to have developed from the indigenous cat of Great Britain.

PROS AND CONS

Plus Points
- Sweet-natured and even-tempered

- Short-coated and do not shed too much fur

- Generally undemanding

- Quiet voiced

- Do not very much mind being left alone

- Often happy to be a sole cat

- Playful as kittens, but generally much less so as adults

Minus Points
- The short coat is thick and dense, requiring regular daily grooming

- Can tend towards gluttony and, thus, obesity; keep an eye on their diet

- Tend to be lazy

This Blue and White Bi-colour kitten shows almost perfectly matched markings, the correct standard for the G.C.C.F.

Smokes, with their pale undercoats, display a colour or pattern on only about three-quarters of the hair shaft. They are available in many colours, including (left) tortie and (right) black.

Colourpointed British are available in just as many colours and patterns as the Siamese. This is a Chocolate Colourpointed.

British Whites may have three different types of eye colour and can be blue-eyed, orange-eyed or, as shown here, odd-eyed.

Tabbies are one of the oldest-known patterns of cat and are available in a wide range of colours – many people consider the Silver Tabby to be the most elegant.

Self colours are perennially popular and there is always a good turn-out of Creams at any cat show.

Another cat native to Britain is the Manx from the Isle of Man. For perfection, it should be completely tailless and this fine White shows off the standard well.

Foreign Breeds

This group includes a great variety of different breeds, mainly shorthairs but some with longer coats. They all have distinct looks, temperaments and needs and so if an outgoing and interesting pedigree cat is what you are after, this could be the right place to look.

●

There are not only some well-known, established breeds within this group, but also some newer varieties that have been purpose-bred for their looks and temperaments. In general, they are more outgoing than Persians and British, but not usually so noisy and demonstrative as the Burmese, Siamese and Orientals.

PROS AND CONS

Plus Points

- Intelligent and playful
- Need little extra grooming – once a week is enough
- Companionable and interesting to live with
- Very playful and active (boisterous even)
- Available in all sort of shapes, sizes, colours and fur texture
- Like to be part of the family
- Some of the less furry breeds may be suitable for owners with breathing complaints
- Usually good with children (as long as they are gentle)

Minus Points

- Can be noisy
- Do not like to be in an 'over-catted' household, but do not like being alone
- May take time to be at ease with other pets
- Some varieties prefer a quiet, childless home

The Abyssinian is an old, established breed, so named as it was thought to have originated in what is now known as Ethiopia. It is available in many colours; this Blue is a more recent addition.

The Bengal is another of the newer 'man-made' varieties and was created to produce the colour and pattern of the Asian Leopard Cat, with the size, temperament and personality of the domestic cat. Available in several colours, they are either spotted, as illustrated, or marbled.

Originally the result of an accidental mating in London between a Chinchilla and a Lilac Burmese, the Burmilla is now a well-established breed in its own right. It is available in several colours, as well as the Self, known as a Bombay, and the Tiffanie, a Semi-Longhair equivalent.

The result of natural mutations, curly-coated cats have been found in several parts of the world. Probably the two best known are (right) the Devon Rex and (below) the Cornish Rex.

The Japanese Bobtail,
known as the Mi-Ke
in its native Japan, is
considered to be a
symbol of friendship
and hospitality.
Popular in the United
States, it has only
recently arrived in
Britain where it is
still extremely rare.

The Ocicat (above) is another 'man-made' breed designed to resemble a wild cat, but, unlike the Bengal, it does not have any wild blood in its ancestry. It arrived by way of a breeding plan designed to produce a Siamese cat with Abyssinian points.

The Korat is an ancient breed, originating in Thailand. It is a blue-only variety with a distinctive heart-shaped face.

The Russian Blue is thought to have been brought to Europe and Britain by seamen leaving the north Russian port of Arkhangelsk. Indeed, it was originally called the Archangel cat. It has a following on both sides of the Atlantic.

Native to Singapore, where it was considered the 'street cat', the Singapura was taken to the United States, where a breeding programme was established. One of the smaller varieties of cat, it is rapidly gaining popularity and is very intelligent, friendly and playful.

Often thought to be hairless, the Sphynx (facing page) actually has a light, down-like covering of fur. First seen in Canada, as the result of a natural mutation, this breed has a firm following of devotees.

The Tonkinese,
originally developed
by mating Burmese
with Siamese, is now
an established breed
in its own right.
Available in many
colours, including
(below) blue.

A newer variety of cat, relatively uncommon in the U.K., the Snowshoe was developed in the United States by crossing a Siamese with an American Bi-colour Shorthair.

Burmese Breed

These plain- or tortoiseshell-coated shorthair cats may not immediately look as 'pedigree' as their Siamese cousins, but their incredible personality has ensured a firm following among cat lovers.

●

They are not usually so vocal as the Siamese; while they do 'speak', they tend to be like well-behaved children and speak when they are spoken to and rarely initiate a conversation! They are great characters and will love their owners with an almost dog-like devotion, which can be taxing on your time.

PROS AND CONS

Plus Points	Minus Points
• Easy to groom and care for	• Can be noisy (when calling)
• Very friendly and affectionate	• Can be bossy and want to be top cat (or dog!)
• Playful and extrovert – even in old age	
	• Can be territorial towards other animals
• Rarely faddy eaters	
	• Do not like being in an 'over-catted' household
• Highly intelligent	
• Want to be part of the family	• Need a lot of human attention
• Usually get on well with children and other animals	• Can be destructive if left on their own
• Very companionable	

Active, intelligent and playful, the Brown Burmese is the original and best-known colour of this very popular breed.

The Chocolate Burmese(right) was originally developed in the United States, while the Red (left) is a purely British invention.

As with all breeds of cat, the Tortie (facing page) is almost always a female-only variety. Often referred to as 'naughty torties' because of their mischievous nature, these two kittens, a Lilac Tortoiseshell (left) and a Blue Tortoiseshell (right), are no exception.

Siamese Breed

Siamese are probably the most instantly recognizable of all pedigree cats. With their contrasting darker points set off against a pale body colour, they just exude good breeding and elegance.

●

They are extremely popular, but those who have never lived with a Siamese before may find them a little demanding and their loud voices are not to everyone's taste. They are very intelligent and charismatic and few people who have ever been owned by one of these cats would ever look for another breed again.

PROS AND CONS

Plus Points	Minus Points
• Easily groomed, shorthaired coat; the Balinese needs a little more regular grooming	• Very vocal, especially when calling
• Highly intelligent	• Need a lot of attention or they will become bored and destructive
• Make wonderful loving and devoted companions	• Do not like to be left alone and need another feline playmate
• Friendly, playful and outgoing extroverts	• Can sometimes be prone to faddy eating
• Usually good with children and other animals – but on Siamese terms as they do not like being teased and taunted	• Territorial and can be prone to domestic spraying

*In type and
temperament the
Balinese is just like
the Siamese and is
available in just as
many colours and
patterns, the
difference being it has
a silky semi-
longhaired coat.*

*The Seal Point is the
best known and
oldest of all the
Siamese colours.*

The Blue Point, with its glacial-white body and cool blue points, is a popular colour variation.

Siamese are also seen with patterned points, as this Seal Tabby Point displays with dramatic effect.

Oriental Breed

Orientals are basically Siamese-shaped cats without the restricted 'Himalayan' coat pattern.

●

They come with both plain and patterned coats and in a variety of colours. Their temperament and character is just as typically 'Siamese': outgoing, extrovert and highly intelligent.

●

They make wonderful companion pets as, like the Siamese, they love people, but they have all their 'minus' points too, as they are demanding.

PROS AND CONS

Plus Points	Minus Points
• Smooth, shorthaired glossy coats that need little other than 'hand' grooming, except the semi-longhair Angora, which needs regular brushing and combing	• Has the typical 'Siamese' voice and knows how to use it
• Friendly, affectionate and loving	• Does not like to live in an 'over-catted' household
• Loves people and is highly companionable	• May be more prone to spraying than some breeds
• Good with children and other pets, as long as they are prepared to accept the cat's terms	• Does not like being a single cat
• Highly intelligent	• Inclined to be bossy with less assertive breeds
	• Inclined to be territorial

The Havana is probably the best-known of the Self colour Orientals and with its rich, chestnut-brown coat is certainly one of the most appealing.

The semi-longhaired version of the Oriental is known as the Angora. It is available in a variety of colours; this fine Lilac shows the correct, plume-like tail.

Spotted Tabby Orientals are among the most popular within this entire group. This fine example of a Chocolate 'spotty' is a Supreme Grand Champion.

The clearly defined markings on this Oriental Classic Silver Tabby just exude pedigree and good breeding.

7

HEALTH CARE

A healthy, fully inoculated cat should have to see the veterinarian only once a year for the annual booster shots, but accidents and illnesses do occur and you may have to consult him or her as a matter of urgency. Despite their grace and elegance, cats can sometimes be very accident prone and their inquisitive natures often get them into dangerous situations they cannot get out of, resulting in trauma and injury. Equally, while your cat can be immunized against most life-threatening viral infections, there are many other illnesses that cannot be prevented in this way. As a cat grows older, the problem of organ degeneration may also arise. The organs that most often fail in old age are the kidneys, liver and heart.

Many common illnesses can be treated effectively at home, but it is wise to seek your veterinarian's advice first, even if only over the telephone. Do not attempt to treat your cat

SKELETON AND INTERNAL ORGANS OF THE CAT

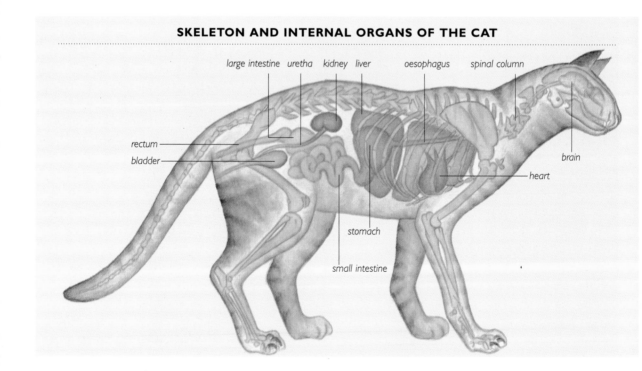

large intestine   uretha   kidney   liver   oesophagus   spinal column

rectum

bladder

brain

heart

stomach

small intestine

yourself unless you are completely certain of the diagnosis and fully confident of the procedure. Never give cats medication designed for humans.

Conventional veterinary treatments are the norm and usually the most effective. However, there is now a growing trend, as there is with human illnesses, to turn towards alternative remedies. The best known and most frequently used of these is probably homeopathy and there are some veterinarians who are also homeopathic practitioners.

There is certainly a place for alternative therapies and most veterinarians will be happy to discuss them with you and, where needed, refer you to a qualified specialist.

ALTERNATIVE THERAPIES

Dietary Control

Commercial cat food manufacturers are turning more towards specific dietary requirements – and with good reason. Low-fat and low-cholesterol foods reduce the chance of heart problems and a diet low in magnesium can significantly improve the well-being of a cat with kidney problems.

Homeopathy

Homeopathy deals with the whole body system, not just the specific complaint. For this reason it is most important to have not only the correct diagnosis, but also full details of the cat and its behaviour. As there are no known side effects, this is a gentle way of treating some complaints and can often be successful in an older cat or one suffering from allergies.

Herbalism

The curative use of plant extracts is one of the oldest of medical treatments and, as with homeopathy, is unlikely to cause unpleasant side effects. Herbal preparations are readily available and usually come in two forms. Most good pet shops stock a wide range of herbal pills specially prepared for animals. Similar herbal remedies are made for humans, but they will not be so 'cat palatable' and dosages may be inappropriate. Liquid preparations are also available; the only drawback to these is that they are distilled in brandy and most cats hate the taste.

Acupuncture

All animals, including humans, have meridians along which their energy is channelled. These can become unbalanced through injury or illness but a skilled acupuncturist can correct this by the manipulation of tiny needles in the appropriate meridial nodes. Acupuncture is known to be particularly effective with joint problems, such as arthritis, and also with skin allergies, kidney problems and general metabolic disorders.

Aromatherapy

The use of essential oils has known benefits to humans, but it is only recently that they have been used to treat cats. These are naturally occurring substances derived from the flowers, bark, leaves, roots and fruits of many plants. As they are very potent, only a few drops of any oil are used and all oils must always be diluted before application. They are exclusively for external use. Several oils, such as lavender and

Bach Flower Remedies

These are made from infusions of various flowers in water preserved in alcohol. Rescue Remedy, a combination of five other remedies, was designed for treating shock and extreme stress. Intended for human treatment, Rescue Remedy can also be given to cats to relieve the symptoms of trauma. A dispensing dropper is supplied with the bottle and one or two drops can be put directly on the cat's tongue for instant effect in an emergency. For longer-term use, add a couple of drops to the water bowl each day.

tea tree, have antiseptic properties and may be used to soothe and cleanse slight injuries. Others are good for treating skin conditions or muscular strain and there are some whose aroma is naturally tranquillizing and effective in treating nervous or travel sick cats. Lavender oil may also be used as a non-chemical alternative for getting rid of fleas.

Physiotherapy, Osteopathy and Chiropractic

The use of gentle but firm manipulation can be especially beneficial to a cat suffering from arthritis or rheumatism or one that has suffered from a skeletal injury or muscular strain.

Healers

No one knows how or why some people seem to have a special power to heal, usually without even touching the patient – human or feline. It has been suggested that energy of some kind is transferred from healer to sufferer and people who have experienced it have described sensations of strength, tingling and warmth. It can be very effective and has no known side effects on cats.

Animal Behaviourists

Some clinical disorders may not respond to conventional or complementary therapies as their causes are psychological rather than physiological. Many veterinarians are now referring their patients to behaviourists who have helped considerably with anti-social problems, such as spraying and aggression (see page 59), skin disorders and other ailments.

FIRST AID

If you can, consult your veterinarian before doing *anything* to your cat; it is often possible to do more harm than good. This is not always practicable and, if no veterinary assistance is available, you may have to act quickly. Remember that any sudden trauma may result in shock (see page 116) and the cat should be treated for this as well as the clinical condition it presents.

Bites and Stings

Animal bites: all animals, including humans, carry bacteria in their mouths. Consequently, if your cat has been bitten, it should receive a course of antibiotics to prevent an abscess forming at the puncture site and possibly even septicaemia developing. The wound may also require suturing by your veterinarian.

Bee and wasp stings: external stings usually result in a localized, painful swelling. Applying a cold compress reduces the inflammation and pain. It is important to remove a bee 'sting'; if you can see it (and your cat will allow you), pull it out with a pair of tweezers. If not, you must take it to the veterinarian. If your cat has been stung in the mouth or throat – or has even swallowed the insect – seek urgent veterinary attention, as the resulting swelling could cause the airways to become blocked and the cat to choke. Until you can get to the veterinarian, place a small piece of ice in the cat's mouth and wrap a cold compress (or even a packet of frozen peas!) around the neck.

Snake bites: in some countries snake bites are

rare, as snakes are relatively uncommon. Britain, for example, has only one native venomous breed. Other countries are not so lucky and an inquisitive cat may get bitten. If your cat has been bitten and you are *certain* the snake is not venomous, treat as for any animal bite. If you are unsure or know the snake is venomous, you must get the cat to veterinarian *as soon as possible* so that an antiserum can be administered. Give a good description of the snake, so that he or she will know the correct antiserum to use. If the journey is a long one, you may have to apply a tourniquet above the puncture site to stop the venom travelling further into the cat's system. This should be done in an emergency

only as a last resort. A tourniquet applied by unskilled hands can restrict the blood supply, resulting in tissue death, gangrene and, ultimately, amputation.

Spider bites: some parts of the world, especially in the southern hemisphere, have indigenous spiders that bite. many of which are poisonous. These should be treated in the same way as snake bites and the cat must have *urgent* veterinary attention.

Burns

Burns caused by direct contact with a hot surface and scalding from boiling liquid must be treated quickly. If possible, hold the affected area under cold running water to minimize the

LOOKING AFTER A SICK CAT

This is really a matter of common sense. Treat your cat just as you would an unwell person: provide it with peace and quiet, warmth, a light diet and *most importantly* lots of tender, loving care. If your veterinarian has prescribed a course of tablets, make sure that you follow the instructions; even if the cat seems better, *always* complete the full course of treatment unless your veterinarian has advised otherwise.

Keep veterinary drugs in a cat-proof container. Many are made so cat palatable that the cat actually *wants* to eat them and thinks they are treats.

A hunched posture and a 'staring' coat are often indicative of ill-health.

swelling and reduce the pain and get the cat to the veterinarian as soon as possible. *Never* 'burst' a blister and do not apply any ointments or lotions unless recommended by your veterinarian.

Chemical burns should be treated in the same way, but with added caution. The cat's immediate reaction will be to lick the affected area to soothe and clean itself. This causes further problems: the tongue will be burned, too, and the chemical may also poison the cat. Wrap the cat in a clean, non-fluffy towel or sheet to prevent it licking and take it to the veterinarian *immediately.* If you know what the chemical is, tell the veterinarian and, if possible, take the container with you.

Choking

Cats are not usually as accident prone as dogs when it comes to swallowing things that they should not, but accidents do happen and choking will result if a foreign body sticks in the throat. This might be something that they have been playing with – even some toys sold for cats are not completely 'cat proof' (see Household Hazards page 46). More often it is a splinter of bone that has become lodged in the throat. The cat might also have been stung (see page 112). Contact your veterinarian for advice as soon as possible; preferably take the cat to him or her.

If this cannot be done quickly, you must act: open the cat's mouth and see if you can find what is causing the obstruction. Remove it, if you can. You can also try holding your cat over your shoulder, with its head pointing down, and give it a firm slap on the back, rather like

'burping' a baby, as this might dislodge the offending item. If nothing comes out and the cat is still choking, you must rush it to the veterinarian immediately.

Cuts and Abrasions

Minor cuts and surface skin wounds can be treated quite easily. Apply a cold compress to stem the flow of blood and then clean the wound with a diluted antiseptic that contains no phenols or cresols (both of which are lethal to cats). If the blood flow continues, the wound may need stitching by the veterinarian. If all seems well, let the cat lick the wound clean but keep an eye out for infection, as the cat will then require a course of antibiotics.

Drowning

Always keep ponds or swimming pools covered when a cat is allowed out unsupervised. Cats can swim, but not many are very good at it, so there is a serious risk of drowning if your cat falls in.

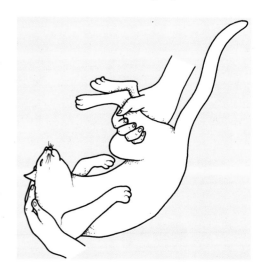

HEALTH CHECK – WHAT TO LOOK OUT FOR

Excessive drinking/urination This is usually associated with kidney problems.

Limping This is usually caused by a sprain or an injury; in the older cat, it is more likely to be indicative of arthritis or rheumatism.

Lumps, bumps and swellings A fast-appearing swelling is usually an abscess caused by a cat fight, but other swellings may indicate stings, bites, injury or even tumours.

Scratching This may mean the cat has a picked up parasites such as fleas, mites, ticks or ear-mites. Allergies also cause scratching - dermatitis and eczema are two examples – and so does the fungal infection, ringworm. It might also be that the cat has an itch!

Sneezing Often merely an allergy to cat litter, dust or pollen, but sneezing might be symptomatic of the much more serious cat influenza.

Haws Cats have a third eyelid that moves from side to side rather than up and down. A visible or 'raised' haw can indicate general ill-health, but may also suggest conjunctivitis or a foreign body in the eye.

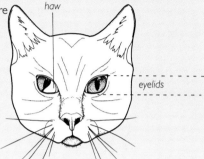

Right is a healthy eye and left shows a 'raised' haw.

haw

eyelids

Act quickly to expel whatever water it has inhaled. Hold the cat downwards and slap it on its back. If this does not work, hold the cat firmly by the back legs, supporting the back of the neck, and swing it downwards (see left). Mouth-to-mouth resuscitation may also be required; use the method applicable to babies.

Electric Shocks

Some cats are just fascinated by wires and cables. Chewing through them while they are plugged in will result in an electric shock. If this happens, *do not touch your cat until you have switched off the appliance* as you will be electrocuted, too. Contact your veterinarian *urgently* and, if he or she cannot see the cat immediately, you will have to act very quickly.

If the cat has stopped breathing and/or there is no visible pulse, start by giving mouth-to-mouth resuscitation, using the technique for a baby or young child. Then apply heart massage, pushing firmly against the cat's chest, just under the sternum (breast bone), where the heart is located. This must be done firmly.

Do not worry that you will injure the cat; to all intents and purposes, it is already dead – but if you can revive it, with little more than a bruise or cracked rib, you have done well.

Fits

Fits may be caused for a variety of reasons. Poisoning (see page 116) is the commonest, but cats can suffer from epilepsy and – in countries where the problem is endemic – rabies. A 'fitting' cat looks quite shocking if you have never seen one before, but it is quite unmistakable: the cat goes into convulsions and sometimes froths at the mouth. As it has temporarily lost muscular control, it is possible that it could further injure itself. To prevent skeletal damage, put the cat on

ROAD ACCIDENTS – HANDLING AN INJURED CAT

It is most important that the cat receives veterinary attention as soon as possible. While there may be obvious external damage, it is quite likely that are internal injuries too.

• Reassure the cat with a soothing voice and

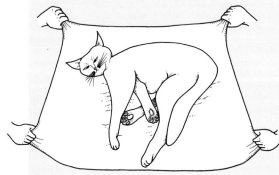

stroke the top of its head *very* gently.
• Handle the cat as little as possible.
• Keep it warm – put your coat or something similar over it, but nothing that is too heavy.
• If the veterinarian is unable to come to the accident (which is likely), make a stretcher out of what you have available, such as a coat or car rug, and slide it *gently* under the cat. If you have something firm that is cat-sized, such as a tray or rigid board, ease the cat onto it for extra support.
• Never let the cat dangle and, if possible, keep the head slightly lower than the body to increase the blood supply to the brain, thus lessening the chances of brain damage.
• Keep the cat warm, quiet and reassured while in transit to the veterinarian.

a soft surface, such as a carpeted floor. As the cat may swallow or bite its tongue, place something like a pencil across the jaw (do not use your finger if rabies is a possibility).

Fits are usually 'one off' events but, if the cat persistently convulses, it may be epileptic, and you veterinarian will prescribe a suitable course of anti-convulsants.

Poisons

Cats may be poisoned by ingesting a toxic substance or by absorbing it through their paw pads. If you suspect that your cat has been poisoned, contact your veterinarian *as soon as possible*. If the poison is known to you, tell him exactly what it is or, even better, take the

container along with you.

If treatment is delayed, you will have to act quickly. If you know the cat has swallowed a poison, give it an emetic made up from a strong solution of salt and water. This will make it vomit and stop the poison spreading further into the system. A word of warning: if you know that the poison swallowed is *caustic* do not encourage vomiting, as this can cause even more damage.

Shock

After suffering a traumatic injury, your cat will probably be in shock. Keep it quiet, warm and comfortable. Talk to it in kind, reassuring tones; it needs to hear a comforting, familiar voice.

This is a time when homeopathic and herbal

treatments really show their efficacy, so it is sensible to be familiar with them. A good stand-by to keep in the First Aid box is Bach's 'Rescue Remedy' (see page 111) It has an almost instant effect and is just as useful for traumatized cats as it is for humans.

Stuck up a Tree

Cats sometimes get themselves into situations from which they cannot escape. The commonest is getting stuck up a tree. When they realize they do not know how to come down, they climb higher and higher – where the branches are thinner and thinner. If you are going to try to get the cat down by using a ladder, remember that it will be frightened and may fall before you can reach it or the branch may break.

Although cats are reputed always to land on all four paws, the impact of landing (especially on a hard surface) can cause a fractured jaw and internal injuries. Be prepared to 'break' its fall and, before taking any radical action, get some help from your family or neighbours – you will need four of them! Position a duvet or sturdy blanket, with a person holding each corner, as a 'safety net' and, with luck, you cat will not suffer too much from its ordeal! Always try to remain calm throughout this procedure, as any shouted instructions will further panic the cat.

COMMON AILMENTS

These all require a proper veterinary diagnosis – some more urgently than others. If you explain the symptoms clearly to your veterinarian, he or she will be able to tell you how urgent it is to see the patient.

Many ailments respond well to a short course of antibiotics, while others may require longer treatment. Your veterinarian may even suggest that alternative or complementary treatments are more appropriate for some problems. *Never* attempt to treat a cat without consulting your veterinarian first and *never* use human drugs, such as aspirin, as they can be lethal to a cat.

Abscess

This is most usually seen after a cat has been in a fight, but can also be caused by a local infection, such as an impacted tooth. It usually results in a localized swelling that causes pain and it should be treated by your veterinarian.

Usually a subcutaneous injection of antibiotic is followed up by a course of tablets. An untreated abscess may result in septicaemia, so it is important for treatment to start as soon as possible and for the full course to be given.

Acne

Usually seen in adolescent cats, feline acne is most commonly found around the mouth and chin. In minor cases it causes only blackheads and pimples, which can be easily treated with an appropriate lotion. More severe cases can result in an abscess and so the cat will need a course of antibiotics prescribed by the veterinarian.

Feline Infectious Leukaemia Virus

This is sometimes, mistakenly, called feline AIDS. Although the FeLV virus destroys the cat's immune system and has some similarities to HIV (human immuno-deficiency virus), the two are not interactive. You cannot catch AIDS from your cat. A cat diagnosed as FeLV positive can infect other cats, but is not necessarily under a death sentence itself. What kills such a cat is a secondary illness developed as result of its failed immune system. A vaccine is available (see page 45).

A tree collar, made from wire mesh, can be fixed to the trunk to prevent your cat from climbing dangerously high.

Anaemia

Lethargy, pale gums and tiredness can all be symptoms of anaemia, a disorder that results in the red blood cells not supplying enough iron to the organs. It may be caused by a deficiency in the cat's diet. There is also an infectious form of anaemia, known as FIA (feline infectious anaemia). They both require veterinary attention but different forms of treatment.

Anal problems

A pair of glands is situated either side of the anus and these can become infected. Usually, a cat with this problem will be seen to be 'dragging' its bottom along the ground, as if to relieve an itch. The glands can be expressed by gently squeezing them with cotton wool soaked in warm water. Be warned that what comes out has a pretty horrible smell! If the glands become impacted, this will often cause an anal abscess to form. This can usually be cleared up with a course of antibiotics but, if the problem is severe and recurring, your veterinarian may suggest that the anal glands are surgically removed.

Another, less common, problem is an anal prolapse. This looks rather like a raspberry extending from the cat's anus and can be quite frightening if the owner has never seen this condition before. It is often caused by a diet with insufficient roughage. It is important that the cat receives veterinary attention as soon as possible.

The anal glands are situated either side of the anal sphincter.

Allergies

Allergies seem to be on the increase; this is not just seen in humans, but also in our pets. It is more evident in urban areas and may be linked to environmental pollution. Skin, eye and breathing problems are among the most frequently seen allergic reactions. Also the current trend in adding colourings and preservatives to food can cause both behavioural and digestive disorders. As there might be an underlying clinical disorder, always contact your veterinarian for a correct diagnosis. If it does prove to be an allergy, you may find that an alternative or complementary treatment is recommended, such as homeopathy or herbalism, as these often work with allergies better than conventional drugs.

Arthritis

Most usually seen in the older cat, this causes the affected joint to stiffen and sometimes swell, often resulting in lameness. Most often it is the result of simple wear and tear on the joints, but there can be other causes, such as an unbalanced diet. Treatment depends on how severely the cat is affected. In mild cases, it may be as simple as changing its food, but if the cat shows more severe problems, it may have to be put on a course of steroids or anti-inflammatory drugs. It is not unusual for modern veterinarians to suggest acupuncture, homeopathy or herbalism to sort this problem out.

Constipation

A cat that frequently strains on its litter tray is probably suffering from constipation. This is most often caused by a lack of fibre and so the diet should be adjusted. A furball (see page 120) may also be the cause. Your veterinarian will usually recommend liquid paraffin; one

If you are in any doubt about your cat's condition, always consult your veterinarian for an accurate diagnosis.

cat has a furball (see page 120), but if an otherwise healthy cat suddenly develops a cough it may have something lodged in its throat and this requires urgent action so that it does not choke (see page 114).

Cystitis and Bladder Problems

Cystitis is an infection often thought of as a 'female-only' problem, but male cats can suffer from it, too. The most usual symptom is that the cat is seen to strain when on its litter tray; this may also be accompanied by blood-tinged urine. Your veterinarian will be able to prescribe a course of antibiotics to clear up the problem.

In some cases, cystitis may be caused by the cat's urine being too alkaline; this could be due to diet and your veterinarian will suggest the most suitable foods. Alternatively, it may be due to kidney problems for which he or she will be able to suggest an appropriate treatment.

Dandruff

Skin naturally sheds dead cells and some animals shed more than others. A build-up of this is known as dander or dandruff. It may be aggravated if the skin is too dry, in which case changing the diet to include more oily foods will result in an improvement. While grooming is essential to keep the fur and skin in good condition, it is possible to over-groom, resulting in dandruff, as the skin has been over-stimulated and so produced more cells. If the condition persists, contact your veterinarian, as there may be a more serious dermatological problem. If you are suffering from a skin rash, your cat may have skin mites and has transferred them to you.

teaspoon a day is the usual dose. Persistent constipation should be investigated, as there may be an intestinal blockage or other serious condition, which requires urgent attention and, usually, surgery.

Conjunctivitis and Eye Infections

The eye is a delicate organ which is easily damaged. If it is weeping or the haw (see page 115) is 'up', consult your veterinarian, as urgent treatment may be required. If you have more than one cat, it is likely to be a simple traumatic injury caused by over-exuberant playing, but it could equally be symptomatic of one of the cat 'flu viruses or chlamydia (see page 44).

Coughs and Colds

Cats presenting these symptoms have usually contracted one of the cat 'flu viruses (see page 44), which attack the nose and upper respiratory tract. Persistent coughing may suggest that the

Giving medicine

Some owners will find it a relatively simple task to pop a pill down their cat's throat, but some cats are more difficult to handle.
• Crush the pill and mix it in a *small* quantity of a favourite food.
• Coat the pill in a little butter or cheese, if your cat likes it.
• Try a pill 'popper', a syringe-like device available from pet shops.

If you persistently have problems in adminstering medication, chat with your veterinarian; it is becoming increasingly common for antibiotics to be produced in a paste form which is much easier to use.

Diarrhoea

This is often caused by a cat's eating something that has resulted in an imbalance in the digestive system causing a stomach upset. Try starving your cat for 24 hours, allowing it to take only pure water and natural live yogurt. This will often sort out this problem, as it will restore the natural bacterial balance. If the problem persists for longer, seek veterinary advice as it may indicate a more serious problem, such as enteritis, that requires treatment.

Ear Problems

If a cat persistently scratches its ears, it probably has ear mites (see page 40). It might also be caused by a foreign body, such as a grass seed. Consult your veterinarian, as these conditions are exceedingly irritating for the cat. Ear mites are treated with veterinary ear drops and a foreign body will have to be removed; in the case of grass seed, before it starts to germinate.

Furballs

This is a common condition, but one that your cat is unlikely to suffer from if it is regularly groomed. As cats are such clean creatures, they groom frequently and, if there is any loose fur in their coats, it will be ingested, leading to the formation of a furball. A dose of liquid paraffin, one teaspoon twice a day, should sort out the problem. However, it would be better to groom your cat regularly to prevent this condition.

Fur Loss and Eczema

There are many reasons why a cat might lose some of its fur and this, accompanied by itchy skin, is generally described as eczema. One of the commonest causes, especially in the summer, is allergic reaction to flea bites (see page 45). If the fur loss is confined to small areas, especially around the back of the head and spine, and the skin appears sore and flaky, it could indicate ringworm, a contagious zoonosis that needs urgent veterinary treatment. Contact dermatitis, especially around the neck, can be caused by chemically-impregnated flea collars. Sometimes a hormonal imbalance, often caused by a cat being neutered at too young an age, may give rise to fur loss problems; your veterinarian may suggest a course of hormone replacements. Most cats love a warm place to sleep; cats that spend a lot of time sleeping on a radiator, the top of a central heating boiler or on a heated cat pad may well end up with an almost bald stomach!

Haematoma

A haematoma (below) is a blood-filled eruption (unlike an abscess, which is filled with pus). It usually appears on the ear after a serious cat fight. If left untreated, it may result in a 'flop' ear,

a permanent condition often seen in 'battle-scarred' tom cats. The sooner it is treated, the less likely it is that your cat will be scarred for life.

Heart Disease and Stroke

While some conditions are congenital and can affect a young cat, most heart problems are associated with increasing old age. This is another good reason why, as your cat gets older, it should have regular veterinary check-ups.

A stroke can happen at any time but, like heart disease, is usually associated with advancing years. It is sometimes triggered by shock or bereavement and, if the stroke is mild, the cat will soon learn to cope with its disability.

Heatstroke and Sunburn

Like humans, cats can suffer from heatstroke. The symptoms may range from simple twitching to a more serious fit (see page 115). In mild cases, it can be helpful to immerse the cat's paws in cold water, as this will quickly lower the body temperature and give almost instant relief.

With global warming, all animals are becoming more prone to sunburn which can lead to skin cancer. This is more prevalent in cats with little fur, such as Rex and Sphynx, and those with pale-coloured fur and little skin pigmentation to protect them from harmful rays. Many veterinarians now recommend the use of a sun block for cats that are allowed out in the full sun and will suggest a suitable preparation.

Teeth Problems and Gingivitis

Most teeth and gum disorders arise from the cat eating too much 'soggy' food. The importance of

Tooth problems may develop at any age, but are most common in the elderly cat.

a proper, balanced diet, including something hard to exercise and clean the teeth and gums, is of paramount importance (see pages 26–28). This, combined with the use of feline toothpaste and plaque inhibitors (see page 40), will help prevent these problems developing. Prevention is always better than cure and cheaper than veterinary dental treatment.

Vomiting

A cat quite often knows better than we do and will eat grass as an emetic (see page 62). This makes it vomit, naturally cleaning out the digestive system and ensuring a correct bacterial balance in the intestines; it is nothing to worry about. There are other causes of vomiting, such as a foreign body stuck in the throat (see page 114). Persistent vomiting should always be investigated by your veterinarian.

Toxoplasmosis

This is a protozoan zoonosis that can by passed by animal faeces to humans. It is usually associated with dog excreta but it is possible for cats to be infected. The main risk is to pregnant women, as toxoplasmosis can cause foetal deformities, such as deafness and blindness. The risk is small, but any risk should be taken seriously. As most responsible people exercise a normal regime of household hygiene, the risk is minimal. Some doctors recommend that any cats in the household should be re-homed, which is plainly ridiculous. However, it is sensible to wear rubber gloves when changing the litter tray.

INDEX

Page numbers in *italics* refer to captions to illustrations

AUTHOR'S ACKNOWLEDGEMENTS
My grateful thanks to my editor Linda Doeser, designer Pedro Prá-Lopez,
veterinary consultant John Oliver BVETMED, MRCVS and illustrator
Samantha Elmhurst. Thanks also to Murray Thomas for advice and
assistance with computers, my photographic processors Colour Centre
(London) for processing my films with their usual care and efficiency
and Aquapets, Ealing for supplying the accessories for photography.